KW-003-097

I WANT TO GO HOME

I WANT TO GO HOME

Catherine Jacobs

The Book Guild Ltd
Sussex, England

ROCHDALE LIBRARIES	
B JAC	
1098430	
Bertrams	03.07.05
	£16.95
	✓

First published in Great Britain in 2005 by
The Book Guild Ltd
25 High Street
Lewes, East Sussex
BN7 2LU

Copyright © Catherine Jacobs 2005

The right of Catherine Jacobs to be identified as the author of
this work has been asserted by her in accordance with the
Copyright, Designs and Patents Act 1988.

All rights reserved. No part of this publication may be
reproduced, transmitted, or stored in a retrieval system, in
any form, or by any means, without permission in writing
from the publishers, nor be otherwise circulated in any form
of binding or cover other than that in which it is published
and without a similar condition being imposed on the
subsequent purchaser.

Typesetting in Times by
SetSystems Ltd, Saffron Walden, Essex

Printed in Great Britain by
CPI Bath

A catalogue record for this book is
available from the British Library

ISBN 1 85776 925 2

Dedication

*My thanks to my late parents,
to whom I owe everything, and to
the remaining members of my original
extended family, and old friends.
Also to my husband, daughters and
grandchildren, who, as part of my new
extended family, show the unity,
support and love which gives me the
wonderful feeling of déjà vu and
great joy.*

CONTENTS

PREFACE

When the idea of writing this book first came to mind it was simply because when I was a child I always wanted to go home. Nothing more complicated than that.

As I remembered the various occasions when this was obviously important to me, I became increasingly aware of the changes which have had an effect on social issues during this period.

In the majority of cases the changes have been a great improvement on past practices. Most were necessary, but I suggest a few have been to the detriment of some of our previously held views on what family life should be. The argument for or against too much intervention or lack of it by authoritative power interests me and I have tried to introduce some of these social changes into the book. But it is for the reader to ascertain the benefits or otherwise. The book is intended to be a little light reading, even thought-provoking, not a heavy moralistic tome.

1

Please Take Me Home

'Home' refers in this narrative to the first house in a row of ten terraced houses in a street in East London. The street joined the main road, which was a continuous line of small privately owned shops whose owners mostly lived above their businesses.

On the corner where the street joined this main road was a baker's shop, a three-storey building comprising the shop and two floors of living accommodation above. At the rear of this building was a long wall which was the flank wall of further single-storey buildings housing the bakery, store-rooms and garage and continued even further to enclose the remainder of the very long garden.

In the main road next to the baker's shop was the post office and then came the doctor's surgery. The gardens of these properties were also very long, but eventually the first house in the street was reached. The depth of this house and its back garden was the width of these three business premises.

The house had a wide side entrance with high gates. The front half of the side entrance was uncovered but the rear was covered and therefore very useful. When the weather was not suitable for drying the washing in the open air, it could all be hung out to dry under cover.

The house had three rooms upstairs and three rooms downstairs. Downstairs, the building extended further at the back into the garden and accommodated a large room, always referred to as the wash-house, which had originally housed a built-in copper heated from beneath by solid fuel.

As well as the copper there was a large deep sink, a mangle, a table and, when I lived there, shelves which were always filled to capacity with packets of washing powder, soap, starch etc. My mother never 'ran out' of anything.

Over the years changes took place. The brick-built copper was removed and replaced by a gas-heated boiler and eventually a washing machine was installed.

Also housed in this protrusion to the downstairs of the building was the toilet, which, like the laundry room, had its entrance in the garden.

In latter years my parents often considered converting this large room into a bathroom and/or a utility room. It would have been a very simple task, just a door put in the wall separating it from the kitchen. But the original lay-out was so convenient, it never seemed worth the effort. They never needed a bathroom, with so many public baths nearby (more of that later), and it was already being used as a utility room.

The house and garden were not overlooked. It was very private. It had a perfect position considering it was in a busy built-up area in London.

My paternal grandfather and his family lived in this house. He was a bootmaker. This is documented on my parents' marriage certificate.

As a child I was not aware of this but I would sit watching my father when he repaired our shoes, fascinated by the dexterity which he displayed when performing this task. He would explain how it was necessary to shave the leather sole carefully at the edge all round to neaten it, but not at the front of the sole 'because the toe of the shoe gets a lot of wear'. Then he would melt the tip of the brown or black stick of colouring and carefully smear the appropriate colour to the remaining edge of the shoe repair.

2

I have often wondered how my father came by the upright piece of tree trunk, on top of which was fixed a last, where he would fit a shoe when repairing it. I suppose there were various sizes of lasts, because I have seen him repair his own shoes, my mother's, brother's and mine. This was not my father's trade but he was an extremely practical man and could turn his hand to most tasks. Although only nine years of age when his father died, maybe he had seen him at work – maybe my father appeared interested and was encouraged to assist him, eventually to inherit the lasts and tree trunk base.

My paternal grandmother must have been 'handy with a needle', as the saying goes, because not many years ago when I occasionally went with my mother to visit my father's oldest sister, who by then was well into her eighties, she would reminisce about her early life. Always she would relate to me how on Sundays and special occasions her younger brothers and sisters would 'look a picture' in their sailor dresses and suits, boater hats and dainty boots which her parents had made for them. Mother made the clothes, father made the shoes.

In April 1915 my grandfather died aged forty-seven years. He was not a casualty of the First World War, he died of pneumonia as did many others all those years ago. He left behind his widow and seven children. The youngest child was one year old and the oldest was eighteen (the afore-mentioned aunt). My father was the middle child of the seven. He was ten years of age. There were two who were already out to work, one almost ready to leave school and four younger.

How were Grandmother and her children to survive?

The Welfare State as we all know did not arrive until 1948 and it had been a long, arduous journey to reach it.

In 1911 there appeared a National Insurance scheme to provide a source of non-means-tested basic income during

3

interruptions in earning capacity caused by sickness and (to a lesser extent) unemployment, but there was still no mention of widows or children of deceased fathers being given a pension in a comprehensive scheme.

By the time my grandfather died, sick benefit took care of doctors' bills and also provided family support while the wage-earner was sick, but we must remember this particular man (my grandfather) was not sick but dead and there was no automatic pension for his widow and dependants.

But other improvements were transpiring. Health work by local authorities was on the increase. One important step forward was school medical inspections.

Over the years great progress was made and by 1965 a widow in my grandmother's circumstances would have been in receipt of a widow's pension, children's special allowances and a death grant.

However, I have been reliably informed that in my grandmother's situation she would have received nothing. She was left to decide what to do with herself and seven children to support, two of whom were already working but, at eighteen and sixteen years of age, hardly in a position to earn adults' salaries.

After much thought and soul-searching Grandmother (known as Little Nanny) decided to find work that would fit in with her particular family requirements. The early morning was not too much of a problem. The two wage earners were capable of overseeing the needs of the younger siblings. Four were school age, which meant that they were taken care of during school hours in term time. That left only the youngest needing full-time care. Little Nanny needed employment which allowed her to be back home by early afternoon and for the remainder of the day. Who required staff to work only early in the day?

She came up with the idea of cleaning the wards in the local hospital. After all, we are all familiar with hospital routine beginning at the crack of dawn. Who among the majority of the population is not au fait with the desire to go on sleeping when woken up early during a stay in hospital.

She made an appointment to see the matron. She wanted to be seen to do the thing 'properly' as she put it.

The appointed time arrived and she met the matron. She always said in later years that she had been very impressed with the amount of time that the matron spent with her. It appears she went into every detail of Little Nanny's sad situation. She commented on my grandmother's slender figure and asked about her health.

At the end of this long interrogation matron decided that Little Nanny would be given employment commencing the following Monday, on condition that she put her two youngest children into some kind of institution to be cared for until they were a little older. She even helped my grandmother by suggesting an institution with which she herself was familiar.

Home went Grandmother. What a situation to be in. The employment was just what she was looking for: an early start in the morning, but home for lunch and there to care for her children for the remainder of the day and night. But for this she must sacrifice her family unity. She also still had the problem of what to do with the baby all day if she did not take the employment offered but tried looking for other work.

In those days relatives and neighbours were often ready to assist in times of need. Mothers at that time did not work outside the home as much as they do now. Without the domestic appliances which we all now possess, it must have been full-time employment coping with the household chores. So, if a mother was caring for her own family during the day perhaps coping with another mother's offspring too was not impossible when necessary.

During the four days between the interview with matron and the Monday when her employment could commence, Little Nanny somehow was able to resolve the situation to her own satisfaction with offers of assistance. She was content with the solution. She was not prepared to put her two children into an institution and thereby split up her family. But she was very aware of the matron's final condition of employment: children still at home – no job.

Monday morning Grandmother arrived at the hospital very early and she was taken into the matron's office.

She always said that she just stood there facing matron, who was sitting behind her desk slowly shaking her head from side to side. After a period of silence matron stood up and said, 'Are the children taken care of?'

Grandmother answered, 'Yes.'

Matron asked if her (the matron's) suggestion had been the solution. When Grandmother answered 'No,' and added that she couldn't do it, she said matron slowly smiled and moved her head slowly up and down this time and said 'I knew that you wouldn't do it.' She then said that Grandmother would be given a chance to see if she could cope with family and work. She added that she still considered Little Nanny perhaps not strong enough for the work expected of her. She gave Little Nanny instructions to go to matron's office every morning before commencing her duties, where she would find a large mug of cocoa and two slices of bread spread with beef dripping which she was to consume before going to the wards to start work.

My mother first knew Little Nanny when the latter was middle-aged and always said that the only reason for her being known as Little Nanny was because my other grandmother was a tall lady. Little Nanny was actually always quite stout according to my mother. I also remember her as being stout, and motherly. Nobody remembers her ever being ill. She died at eighty-eight years of age, very peacefully.

One evening she felt desperately tired, took to her bed and fidgeted before finally settling down. The doctor had been called and he said she was making herself comfortable because her heart was getting weaker. While her children sat talking and waiting in the sitting room, she just died in her sleep.

The hard work of cleaning the hospital wards from 1915 for twenty years obviously did her no harm; in fact she used to say it had been 'the making of her'. She continued her hospital work until she retired at sixty-five years of age, long past the time when she needed to do such arduous work.

The eldest child in Little Nanny's family was eighteen years of age and fortunately a girl – my experience as a mother of two daughters and as a schoolteacher has taught me that young girls are far more organised than young boys. My husband has a theory which he believes explains this. He says boys go through stages: small boys, big boys, young men and adult men, but girls are women from birth. There must be some truth in this theory because haven't we all seen female toddlers strutting around – handbag on arm organising everything and everybody.

And so a routine was established. Little Nanny would trot off to the hospital very early in the morning. The eighteen-year-old and the sixteen-year-old would organise breakfast for the five younger children, see four off to school and the baby safely delivered to a neighbour – no distance, just a few houses away. I imagine most of this would be the responsibility of the eighteen-year-old. All her life she remained very close to her youngest sister, who was the baby at that difficult time. There are people who appear to miss out on a family of their own and instead become the mainstay of other members of the family. So it was with this lady. She married eventually, but her only child was still-born and soon after this loss her husband died. As I have already said, she remained very close to her youngest sister and spent a great deal of her leisure time with this sister's two children – her niece and nephew. Eventually the niece married and, surprise, surprise, when great-nieces and great-nephews arrived my aunt found a use for her talents once again. Actually, when I accompanied my mother on visits to this aunt in more recent times when Auntie was well in her eighties, she would always be visited by a great-niece and great-nephew who would 'pop in' for a lunch-time snack.

Because this family had had to become self-sufficient they of necessity also became very self-reliant, as one would under the circumstances (more of that later). My grand-mother always said that the children were very little trouble. They were all very industrious. The three older boys par-ticularly became quite sought after by local shopkeepers to do work which did not warrant employing full-time employ-ees. This employment not only increased the family income, it instilled in the young men a work ethic and occupied them in their leisure time.

We must remember they were still responsible for pre-paring themselves for work or school every morning, prob-ably having to care for the younger siblings some of the time, as well as earning money for those little 'extras' which must have made a rather difficult existence more endurable. My father's favourite employment while still at school was helping with a pair of horses which were owned by a local businessman. The love of horses remained with him all his life. His first full-time employment on leaving school was with horses, but in what capacity I do not know. It only

8

lasted for one year, and at fifteen years of age he began a different career – more of that later, too.

And so for nearly two years life settled into a routine for this family.

In 1917 the oldest boy reached eighteen years of age and he entered the army, as did most other young men at that time. My grandmother had not only lost his contribution to the family income, she also now had the worry, like so many other mothers, of her son fighting in France. He was a machine-gunner.

The war ended, as we all know, on November 11th in 1918. Not immediately but at a later date my father's brother returned from France. There was great excitement in the family. His mother and six brothers and sisters were overjoyed that he was able to return to them when so many other families were never going to see their fathers, sons and brothers again.

I can imagine the same scene taking place in thousands of homes around Britain – around the world too. There were the families and friends of these men eager to celebrate their return but also wanting to hear of the soldiers' experiences in the trenches. My father's family was no exception. The boys were now around sixteen, fourteen and eight years of age and would question their older brother about life in France. Unlike my mother's family, who were very quick-tempered, my father's family were not so easily roused and the young ex-serviceman did not lose his temper with his younger brothers. My father said that his eldest brother had always been of a rather quiet temperament before going into the army, but when he returned from the war quiet turned to silent and he would not talk about his experiences to anyone. I am told my grandmother would say to the younger boys, 'Leave him alone, he wants to forget it.' Or, 'He doesn't want to remember.'

From the day of his return he complained of feeling unwell. He suffered dreadful headaches. It is not easy for later generations to comprehend why a young man suffering so much did not seek medical attention. Why did his mother not insist that he did so? We must assume the answer to be simply that visits to the doctor at this time were rarities. He was physically a healthy young man. He had survived a war in dreadful conditions. He had returned to his family prepared to begin again where he had stopped his normal life to fight, and I have been told he resumed his employment with his previous employer.

However, the headaches, the 'explosions' and terrible noises in his head took their toll and he withdrew into himself. He would often take to his bed, his explanation being that when asleep he couldn't hear the 'bangs' in his head.

One morning my uncle complained of feeling unwell and Little Nanny advised him to return to his bed, which he did. She went off to the hospital to work. One can only imagine how worried she must have been. Her eldest son did not appear to be improving. One wonders whether or not she knew of any other soldiers who had returned and were suffering in the same way. Perhaps in her situation, leading such a busy life with work and family, she had little time available to socialise and thereby gain such information.

At the beginning of the twenty-first century it is difficult for us to see in the mind's eye how parochial life must have been not a quarter of the way into the twentieth. This was the era of the extended family. One did not have to travel very far to see close relatives and even not-so-close relatives, which was convenient because private transport was accessible to very few. The time when the majority of families own a car was still a long way away.

10

The majority of the population concerned themselves only with what was going on in their immediate area. For four years they had participated in a world war and were trying hard to settle back into normality. The main means of mass communication – radio and television – had not arrived. It is difficult for us today not to be aware of what is taking place in other parts of our country and also all over the world. We are bombarded with news from the media all day. After the First World War the newspaper was the only way of obtaining news.

This particular day, when my grandmother had gone to work leaving her son in bed, was one she never forgot. She returned home from work and commenced her usual routine, heating the water to have a complete wash. 'All over,' she would often say, 'because you need it after scrubbing and polishing those wards.' Then she would sit down to her lunch. This would often consist of a small tin of red salmon (she would not eat pink) and bread and butter, followed by one or two pastries from the bakery on the corner of the street. My mother, who went to live upstairs in the house when she married my father, told me of this little lunch-time ritual.

But this day she did not even have time for the wash when her son entered the kitchen. He told her how pleased he was to see her safe and sound because he had had a dreadful dream in which he had killed her. I find it difficult to picture the effect it must have had on her, but it must have been exceptional because her life had not been lacking trauma. She told my mother in later years that it terrified her to such an extent that she could hardly cope until early that evening when the doctor opened his surgery.

Nowadays, when most households possess a telephone, someone in this situation will pick up the receiver, dial the surgery number and make an appointment to see a doctor, albeit the appointed time may be days ahead. But this was not so in my grandmother's lifetime, and until at least the 1960s it was customary for one to just arrive at the surgery during surgery hours and wait your turn to see the doctor. It was usually a one-man practice; occasionally there were two doctors. This meant the doctor more often than not would see patients in the surgery and be on call twenty-four hours a day.

I remember as a teenager making one of my rare visits to the doctor. It was early evening, which was the normal time for doctors to open their surgeries, to enable workers to pay a visit on their way home from work. We were all sitting waiting our turn when the doctor hurried through, bag in hand, mumbled an apology, said that he would not be long and went out, presumably on an urgent call to a patient. It was late evening before he returned and resumed his surgery consultations. But at least he did see all of us, and perhaps that is preferable to waiting three or four days for an appointment.

Maybe my uncle had consulted the doctor, at some time since his return from the war because the doctor returned with my grandmother to the house to visit him. Whether or not he knew at the time what the outcome of his visit was going to be, all he said was, 'Yes . . . I think he needs a little rest.' He added that he would make the arrangements for an ambulance to call and collect him the following day.

Fine, everyone was relieved. At last Alfred would have a complete rest, recover and return to his old self. Even the patient himself did not protest. My father said that he appeared drained, completely exhausted. The poor tormented soul was too worn out to care.

The next day arrived and Grandmother prepared him for his journey, sorting out his 'best' clothes. It was important to look nice at a time like that.

The ambulance arrived. Two huge men alighted, wearing white coats. They informed my grandmother her son would not require the clothes and toilet necessities which she had so lovingly packed. Holding him one on each side, they more or less lifted him into the back of the ambulance. My father seemed particularly upset about this. He would always say, 'There was no reason for this, Alf was quite willing to go and able to walk.'

This young man was then taken not to the local hospital but to a mental hospital. That was as far as my father would go when narrating events concerning his brother. What happened after was told to me by my mother. The family was informed that he was suffering from what was then called 'shell-shock'.

For me the poets of that time often give the most vivid descriptions of the horrors of the First World War, particularly Siegfried Sassoon in a poem entitled *They*.

We have all heard of and seen footage of the fighting in the trenches during the First World War. We know of the appalling conditions in which the soldiers had to exist. Just trying to survive in such conditions would be more than enough for most human frames to endure but that was only part of the scenario; there was, after all, a war going on. Fighting, seeing companions killed and maimed and always to the background of incessant shell-fire, it truly must have seemed like 'Hell on Earth'.

We surely should not be surprised that such conditions eventually must take their toll. A period of rest would have benefited many men on whom these conditions were gradually having a debilitating effect. But because the war was claiming so many lives, these men could not be spared from the front lines.

The problem, however, was recognised and psychiatry in the military field began even before the war ended.

The mental breakdowns and nervous disorders were

generically termed 'shell-shock'. By 1916 cases of shell-shock accounted for forty per cent of the casualties in some fighting areas and the army was forced to create treatment centres. However, as far as I know, my uncle was not among those diagnosed.

There were clearing stations established in France and hospitals in Britain. It was not only the lower ranks which were affected, officers too suffered from shell-shock and their treatment was usually more progressive than that administered to the other ranks. However, by 1918 there were in Britain mental hospitals for officers and hospitals for lower ranks.

But as the war receded into the distance, the initial support for the victims of these illnesses gradually waned and access to treatment was negligible other than institutionalisation, which was the fate of some men for many years.

Some people had wanted earlier treatment to be available in ordinary out-patient clinics. This would have alleviated the stigma of mental illness and maybe young men in my uncle's situation would have sought help earlier – who knows?

But progress was made eventually. Too late for my father's brother to benefit although I am certain the authorities and professionals who cared for him administered the treatment which was considered correct at that time.

It was some years later with the Mental Treatment Act of 1930 that the institutions called Lunatic Asylums were renamed Mental Hospitals and mental illness replaced the term lunacy.

Progress continued and by the start of the Second World War in 1939 there were out-patient clinics treating persons with psychological problems. Younger doctors came to recognise the need for psychological training. Doctors began to look at issues which were the early research into

Post-Traumatic Stress Disorder which is now a defined condition.

My uncle began what was to be the rest of his life in the mental hospital. He was not neglected by his family and at least one member of this close-knit family would visit him each Sunday. This would have been impossible a few years earlier when public transport, although known as omnibuses, were pulled by horses, but by 1911 the buses were motorised.

The journey must have been difficult: ten or twelve miles interspersed with bus changes, often waiting for buses in inclement weather. When I listen to persons of that generation it seems that a combination of family love and a strong sense of duty was the mainstay of their existence.

My mother and father began courting and very often would visit my uncle. When the hospital entrance was eventually reached there was a very long drive to the building itself. Transport was provided, or one could go on foot. After their long bus journey, my parents would more often than not enjoy the walk. On the way they would pass low buildings in which were housed other patients, females suffering from a condition which was commonly known then as milk-fever.

Milk-fever was formerly supposed to be due to the over-swelling of the breasts with milk. It could occur at the onset of lactation and was associated with physical and psychological symptoms which included weeping and hysteria. It is not difficult to see why a connection was made between the two happenings.

Now the fever is recognised as puerperal fever and is caused by infection following childbirth. With the use of antibiotics, the risk is all but eliminated. However, in the first quarter of the twentieth century antibiotics were not available, hence the large number of new mothers who suffered infection following the births of their babies and were admitted to mental hospitals. Some of these mothers were in all likelihood suffering from severe postnatal 'blues', which is now a recognised condition too. For others, their symptoms could equally well have been the result of puerperal infection. Unfortunately, some would have been suffering from puerperal psychosis, which is the most severe form of post-natal psychiatric illnesses. It is characterised by thought disorders and severe depression.

Regardless of whether their symptoms were mild or severe the only treatment for some of them appears to have been in mental hospitals.

There are no longer a large number of ladies in mental hospitals suffering from 'milk-fever'. There are no longer large numbers of men suffering from 'shell-shock.' Progress has been made.

Some years went by and Uncle was still hospitalised. On one of their Sunday visits my parents were walking up the long hospital drive, accompanied by other visitors, many of whom they met quite regularly on their visits, when they heard the alarm sounding out loud and clear. Everyone stopped walking and stood quite still for in the distance they could see a man running and being pursued by two others. The chase continued down the hospital drive and my father recognised the escapee as his brother. My father and two other gentlemen who were visiting stopped my uncle and held him until the two pursuing nurses reached the scene.

It is very clear why my father never spoke of this or any further visits to my uncle. What followed must have been extremely traumatic. My uncle went down on his knees, clasped my father round his legs and said, 'Please take me home, Arthur.'

What could my father do but stand by as the two carers took his brother back to the hospital.

The family continued to visit the patient and maybe he derived some comfort from their visits. It was difficult to tell because he never spoke to them again.

My mother informed me that on subsequent visits she and my father would plead with him to talk to them to discuss their wedding plans. They would try coaxing him by telling him of their wish for him to be my father's best man at the wedding. To no avail, he would not speak.

During one of their last visits, while they talked of their wedding, he leaned towards my father, removed my father's trilby hat and put it on his own head. My mother said he then put his head to one side, gave a lovely smile and carefully removed the hat and replaced it on my father's head.

I have often wondered if my father felt himself to blame for his brother's silence. Perhaps he believed that his brother never forgave him for not taking him home. But my father never spoke of it.

My parents were married in June 1927, but my uncle had died in January of that year, aged twenty-seven years.

2

I Want to Go Home

My maternal grandfather died in 1915 and, like my father's father, he too was not a casualty of the First World War but of the dreaded pneumonia. He left a widow and five children whose ages ranged from four to seventeen years. Like my father, my mother was the middle child in the family and she was ten years of age.

The family were not poor. My grandfather, with his two brothers as partners, owned a business which hired out horses and traps, and also what I would venture to call horses and carts, but which were an accepted form of travel at the time. On special occasions the family would travel by this form of transport to such events as the Derby and other well-known horse races.

When Grandfather died it came as a great shock, because as my mother could vividly recall he had been ill but was on the mend and, as the doctor had said, 'The worst is over.' Indeed, Grandfather felt so much better that he asked my grandmother to allow him to polish one of his harnesses while he was still in bed.

My mother was sent to the linen chest to fetch a large white sheet. It was draped over the bed, covering it completely, and Grandfather sat up and polished the harness. The next day, however, he suffered a relapse and died.

The family dropped out of the business, which continued to be run by the two surviving brothers. But there had been a connection with a wood-cutting enterprise also and my grandmother decided to work at this herself. She obviously had to have a source of income. Only one of her children was at work. He was seventeen years of age but the next was only twelve.

It appears to be a fact that both my grandmothers were physically and mentally strong. The newly widowed grandmother began the work of chopping wood and putting it into small bundles which the public purchased to light their coal fires.

She must have continued this for at least twenty years, because I can remember being taken by my mother many times to visit her in her place of work, which was just a few yards off the main shopping centre. I was very young but I remember seeing her sitting behind a very basic piece of apparatus called a tie-horse, in which she would place the approximately eight-inch-long pieces of wood, and fashion them into a bundle and tie with string. Close by, a man would be putting long planks of wood in a position that would enable the mechanical saw to perform its part of the operation. When the wood was in pieces small enough to be chopped, my grandmother and another lady would play their part. I can still smell the wonderful smell of that place – the wood and the sawdust.

Two years later, in 1917, my grandmother remarried. The gentleman whom we knew as Grandad was a very quiet man, the complete opposite of my grandmother, who was a tall, imposing figure of womanhood. She had a very quick temper but was the most generous and kind person, apart from my own mother, that I have ever known. Everyone, it seemed to me, stood in awe of her. Her children, who were adults when I arrived on the scene, were never too old to be reprimanded by her when she considered it necessary.

She was the mainstay of the family and generous to a fault, with love and support for all of us.

Grandmother was known by my immediate family as 'Big Nanny', simply because she was tall and my other grandmother was short, and the person probably who owes the most to Big Nanny is my only remaining aunt, called Eleanor but known as Nellie.

When my grandmother remarried, her new husband was a widower. A few years before, he had married a widow who already had two sons and two daughters. The couple then produced a baby daughter of their own, who was called Eleanor. Unfortunately, the mother died in childbirth. World War One was in progress and the father was in the army. He was left with two stepsons, two stepdaughters and his own baby daughter to bring up. The five children were put in a home.

One often hears institutions of this kind decried and sometimes with some justification but one should remember that, first, there was at the time no way for a father to work, run a home and bring up a young family on his own. Usually relatives assisted: grandparents or aunts and uncles would bring up the children as their own. Second, many of these institutions were run very efficiently. The young people cared for in them were not brought up in opulent surroundings, but neither were many of their peers who were fortunate enough to be living within a family environment.

A sociologist will often document that persons brought up in circumstances such as these children experienced will have no idea of family life and will be emotionally deprived. This was not always so. The baby in this story was brought up in my mother's family (more of this later). The other four young children remained in the 'home', and as each reached the age when they were obliged to leave and go out into the big wide world to earn their own living, he or she went to live with their maternal grandmother, eventually to marry and have very happy family lives of their own.

But to return to Big Nanny and Grandad. They married and my grandmother was taken by her new husband to see his daughter, who by then was two years old. I think it must have been 'love at first sight' for my grandmother and this poor little scrap of a child because to this day Auntie Nellie still never ceases to sing the praises of my grandmother, who she insists saved her life and gave her a home.

My grandmother wanted to take the toddler home to live with the family but was advised by the matron to leave the child in the home. She was a very sickly child who had suffered from mastoid problems and although she was of an age to walk, she showed no signs of doing so. The matron strongly advised my grandmother to re-think her decision because in her opinion the toddler would not live beyond seven years and they would be seven difficult years.

But Grandmother was adamant. The child would join her family.

And so the great day arrived and my mother told me that everyone was extremely excited. Big Nanny loved to see children well dressed and she had had made a pink coat and hat, edged with white fur in which to dress Auntie Nellie for her home-coming. My mother, who was twelve years of age, and her two younger sisters were told that they had bought the little pink shoes for this new family member.

My mothers always remembered the day when the five children waited expectantly for the toddler's arrival. But when she was brought home, to their astonishment she wasn't walking in the new shoes – she couldn't walk properly.

However, with her welfare now assured, she began to

21

improve. As Auntie Nellie even now after so many years will readily admit, my grandmother doted on her and spent a great deal of time taking her to the clinic and the hospital. This was a new experience for Big Nanny, whose own children were extremely robust.

My grandmother must have been a very astute lady, for with all this attention being focussed on the little girl, one would expect to find jealousy in the other siblings. This was not so – they all adored her. The fact that she was and is the calmest, gentlest and kindest of human beings surely must have helped in this situation. She must have appeared to them to be so vulnerable with her real mother dead, but she now had a stepmother and they all had a stepfather and the whole family settled down to normal family life.

The house in which this family lived was unusual. It was in a row of terraced houses but was only attached on one side to the next house. On the further side was a covered entrance about eighteen feet wide with huge double gates which were flush with the fronts of the houses. It was built at the same time as the houses and was attached to both my grandmother's house and the next house. It was, however, part of my grandmother's property, and only the various doors in the side of *her* house led into this covered additional area. It had no rear doors or rear wall and formed the entrance to the back garden.

At the further end of the garden were two huge stables, between which was a space with a staircase to the rear which led up to what was always known in the family as 'the loft'. The loft had doors in the centre front which were permanently kept locked.

The stables and covered side entrance had been very useful when conducting the wood-chopping and horse-and-trap businesses when my grandfather was alive. Now my grandmother decided that as her new husband had taken on the responsibility of her family, it was only fair that she should help supplement the family income. But her newly acquired daughter was only two years old and, with three of her own children still at school, Grandmother was needed at home. So, instead of going out to her daily labour chopping wood, she cleared out the stables and set up her own little enterprise.

With the war over, everyone settled down to a normal family life. The eldest son who had served in the Tank Corps, had been injured and after numerous operations one of his legs was left permanently disabled. Everyone loved having him home, particularly Nellie. She still remembers how she absolutely adored him and how he would sit with her, helping her with school work.

Auntie Nellie to this day is very fond of sausages. One day her mother put this elder son's lunch, which included sausages, on a plate covered by a second plate, ready to be re-heated when he returned from work. When Auntie Nellie came home from afternoon school she could not resist eating one of the sausages from this meal which had been put aside. Uncle returned from work, questioned the short-age and was told by Auntie Nellie that the dog was the culprit. He reminded her that a dog would be unable to replace the top plate. He was extremely angry with her for the first and only time and she has never forgotten it.

This elder son rather took on the role of father to his siblings in the household when discipline was the issue. Grandad was a very quiet gentleman and perhaps felt it wasn't his place as stepfather to make the rules for his stepchildren, particularly as their mother's discipline was always more than adequate.

Grandad was a French-polisher by trade. He was excep-tionally adept at his craft and I am reliably informed he was remunerated well for work undertaken. Consequently, even with the family to support, he was not short of funds for a little recreation. He only had two leisure pursuits. The first was his garden. He was passionate about his runner beans and would sit guarding them from the birds. I have never been aware that birds are particularly fond of runner beans, but it was obviously important to Grandad. His second leisure pursuit was a glass of beer or two or three, or maybe more.

My mother told me that one day she opened the front door to find a lady who lived further down the street. The neighbour asked to speak to my grandmother. When Grandmother arrived on the scene the lady promptly gave her one of those knowing looks which clearly said, 'Do you want *her* to hear?' My mother was sent back to the living-room, where she put her ear to the door to find out what was going on.

She heard the lady say that she had come from the public house just around the corner, where she had seen my grandfather. He was, as she described him, rather merry and in such a generous mood that the Salvation Army lassies who frequented the public houses to give out their literature and collect monetary contributions had been the recipients of at least three ten-shilling notes.

She added that she thought 'his woman' should be informed of this. Hence the visit to Grandmother, who until that moment had been very friendly and polite. She then rose to her full five foot ten and said very curtly, 'I am not his woman, I am his wife. Thank you very much for telling me.' She then shut the door, put on her coat and, of course, her hat, and in a very short time returned with Grandad, who it seems had that morning been paid for work he had completed.

From books I have read and accounts of experiences of times past, it seems that the authorities were less tolerant than the present day powers that be. The policeman on the beat was not a figure to be trifled with by children who were misbehaving or by adults who had consumed a little too much alcohol.

I am afraid Grandad came into the latter category more than once. Some years after this episode he was in trouble again.

He arrived home late one Saturday feeling very sorry for himself, little knowing that Grandmother had already been informed by the wife of his friend that he and the friend had been taken into custody for 'larking about', as he put it, but recognised by everybody else as being 'drunk and disorderly'.

He was to appear in court two days later on the Monday morning, and was distraught. Nothing like that had ever happened to him before – I imagine more by luck than for any other reason.

Was he offered any sympathy by his wife? In a word 'No'. She sent Auntie Nellie to tell my mother, who had just recently married, what had occurred and to inform her that she and the two youngest sisters who were still living at home were going to the coast for a week's holiday. And on the Sunday morning all three set off.

On the Monday evening my mother and father visited Grandad to hear the result of his appearance in court. His punishment had been a very small fine. However, what had upset him more than the fine was a picture postcard which he had received on Monday morning before going to court.

On arriving at their holiday destination the day before, Grandmother had posted a humorous card to Grandad. It depicted a judge with the black cap on his head (denoting the death sentence) saying to a very small terrified man in the dock, 'Have you anything to say before I pronounce sentence?'

My parents thought the whole episode was hilarious and

would often relate the story. It seems when he showed the offending postcard to them he said to my mother, 'Your mother can be very cruel,' and he could not understand why they thought it so funny. When he died twenty-eight years later it was still in his wallet.

Now, with 'women's lib' well advanced and the term 'feminism' generally replacing it, we often hear discussions on the aggressiveness or assertiveness of women. I believe my grandmother definitely fell into the latter category. She was not aggressive but she was assertive, without a doubt, and fair to a fault.

By the time the baby Eleanor (Auntie Nellie) was in junior school she had grown into a healthy happy girl. She had been brought up as one of the family, with the same surname as her father and his wife, whom she thought of as her mother. The other children had a different surname, but as they had a different father that made sense to her.

Until one day in junior school. During a little confrontation with another girl Auntie Nellie said that which young children often will say, 'I will tell my mother.' To which the other child replied, 'She isn't your real mother.'

Auntie Nellie arrived home in tears, desperate to be told that this information was untrue. Grandmother, realising that the child could not be lied to, decided to tell her the truth. She had known that this day would arrive, and she had kept in touch with the whereabouts of the child's real maternal grandmother.

A new routine was then initiated. Eleanor was taken first by my grandmother to visit her real grandmother and then was quite often accompanied by an older sister. Her family gradually grew. As each of the four stepsisters and step-brothers, who had remained in the 'home', reached the age when they had to leave and earn their own living, they went to live with their maternal grandmother. Here, one by one, Auntie Nellie became acquainted with them all.

She has nieces, nephews, great-nieces and nephews, great-great-nieces and nephews. She likes to be kept informed of all family matters and many of us visit, telephone and keep in touch, if only by sending Christmas cards.

As is to be expected, my mother's family in which Auntie Nellie had been brought up were the closest to her. I, as the first grandchild to arrive on the scene when she was only a young teenager, spent a lot of time with her. I am told she would take me out and about from the time I was born. I know I have always loved her very much.

One day when I was very young, probably only two or three years of age, she took me on a visit to another aunt who had recently married. While there I needed the toilet. But I absolutely refused to use my aunt's toilet, stubbornly saying, 'I want to go home.' This resulted in someone going out to locate a taxi, not the easiest of tasks at that time. I was then transported home in grand style and at considerable expense.

My mode of transport home was once again a taxi when for the same reason I wanted to go home while on a shopping trip with Auntie Nellie. On this particular occasion it appears she was struggling to cope with the situation and, not being a very robust young lady, she was noticed by a young gentleman who assisted her by securing the urgently needed taxi.

At that time, and even a generation later when my children were born, it was a combination of parental choice, current trends, routine and the need to use as few nappies as possible which influenced the way toilet-training was practised.

Comparing then and the present day one can see why it was advantageous to get this natural bodily function under control. Then, every nappy had to be washed – no washing machine – and dried – only by hanging on a line in the garden, which was unsuccessful in any but sunny or dry windy weather, or in the house where the atmosphere was warmer. There were not even radiators over which to drape them.

Added to this, there was until recently never a pair of waterproof panties made which prevented the bed from becoming wet. Hence, bed-linen too had to be washed and dried. So from the time of birth it became necessary that the child was toilet-trained as soon as possible.

It followed that any significant, regular event during the day became an occasion when the baby could be put on a potty, with success quite often from the age of a few months. This no doubt was of no great benefit to the potty-training process but it certainly saved the laundering of more nappies.

Now, with washing machines, tumble-driers and extremely efficient waterproof panties, the necessity for early toilet-training is not so urgent. And if the parents so wish, and more and more do so, they do not ever use washable nappies, only disposable ones. I have noticed that in the advice given to new mothers, and young people who will later work with infants, the expected age for this natural function to become controlled is much later than it was in the past.

Today's approach is more sensible than that of the past, which put unnecessary stress on both child and parents and resulted quite often in a child refusing to use somebody else's toilet, which may have been the case with me. But I must admit that it is more than likely that I was merely being uncooperative.

However, although the attitude to this issue now appears

to be an improvement, there is another important part of the baby's life where I believe a retrograde step is being taken. This is the controversial issue of how and when to feed the infant. Should it be on demand, or routine feeding?

When breast-feeding was the norm, it was a compromise. The emphasis was on routine from day one, with complementary feeding only until this routine was established.

Hospital procedure and advice given by child clinics are influenced by the current trend, and now the fashion seems to be for on-demand feeding. This, it is said, will lead to the mother and the baby learning to adapt to each other's ways, and only when the mothers starts to fit in her other activities during the day will the need for routine become apparent. This appears to be a sensible compromise between the on-demand or routine feeding question, just so long as the aim is to have a routine more or less established for when the mother is *obliged* to fit in this time-consuming duty with her other activities.

When a baby is bottle-fed on demand, it must make preparation of the feeds an added difficulty, and why so many mothers choose to bottle feed is a mystery to me. I remember we were once told by a health visitor at an antenatal clinic that cows' milk was meant for baby cows.

Without being too facetious, I wonder if the result of feeding on demand, if taken to the extreme, is seen when infants as young as a few months lie in their baby buggies feeding from bottles which are propped up on pillows. These babies then progress to sitting or walking around holding their own bottles. After this, it seems that children and then adults find it difficult to proceed from point A to point B without drinking on the way. Once they have reached the age when it is legal to drink alcohol, one often sees persons walking about in public doing just that.

Oh! how the Salvation Army must disapprove of such behaviour. From the beginning of their movement the Salvationists worked for moral and spiritual improvement. This was at a time when the excessive drinking of alcohol was the cause of so much misery and poverty within drinkers' families.

The Salvation Army threads its way quite regularly through my tale. Only one member of the family actually belonged to the Salvation Army (more of him later) but I have always been aware of its presence.

William Booth was the founder of the movement, which was originally called the Christian Revival Association. Later it became the Christian Mission and in 1878 the change of name to The Salvation Army came about.

Military terminology followed, a uniform was designed, the bonnet appeared, a flag was used to head street marches and brass bands became a familiar feature.

The mission had begun its work in London. It had soon spread to other parts of the country and by the end of the century it had become an international organisation.

The Salvation Army's influence on social conditions began to be felt in many ways and their concern with the consumption of alcohol continued.

One day my mother's two youngest sisters, who at the time were young teenagers, were out walking when they heard the Salvation Army band in the distance. They naturally stood on the pavement edge to watch it go by, a quite regular occurrence which they would usually enjoy. But not on this particular day because behind the brass band was the usual number of Salvationists escorting a small group of gentlemen, one of whom was Grandad. He and a few friends had presumably been 'rounded up' from a local public house and they were on their way to the Mission Hall to be 'saved'. I think perhaps the Salvation Army 'lassies', as they were called, must have had a special attraction for Grandad, because I wrote of his earlier encounter with them. Perhaps it was their uniform.

Once again, the two girls went immediately to my parents to narrate this sad tale. Once again, my parents could see the funny side of it. Mindful of the fact that Grandad was such a mild, quiet man when sober, they reminded the two girls that his need to be saved from my grandmother might be more important when she was made aware of what had taken place. Is it any surprise that my parents and aunts and uncles were all non-drinkers?

The well-known Congress Hall was in Clapton, a part of Hackney just a few minutes' walk from my home. Its huge, magnificent portico was less than thirty yards from the house in which Auntie Nellie lived for many years.

This building began as the London Orphan Asylum, founded by the Rev Andrew Reed to provide accommodation and assistance to children of respectable professional families where an income was no longer assured due to the death of the father. That was the plight of my parents' families when both my grandfathers died, as already mentioned, and recognised assistance was non-existent.

Clapton and Hackney had been fashionable weekend retreats for wealthy city dwellers, but with London growing so fast at that time, industry and housing began to encroach onto the building's eight acres of land.

In 1866 an outbreak of typhoid prompted the orphanage to look for new accommodation and it moved to Watford in 1870. During its years as the orphanage it had cared for more than four thousand children. It had given a home to more than five hundred girls and boys at any one time.

The building stood empty until 1882 when it was purchased by the Salvation Army which was beginning to rapidly expand and was renamed the Clapton Congress

31

Hall. It was dedicated to the worship of God and the service of man by General William Booth, and opened as a training establishment for Salvation Army officers.

The central quadrangle was roofed over to create a huge amphitheatre which could seat around three thousand people, and for the next forty-eight years the Clapton Congress Hall became the 'Training Garrison' for Salvation Army officers. After their training they were commissioned to preach in all parts of the world.

So, for nearly fifty years, the Clapton Congress Hall was in many ways the focus of the Salvation Army in London. As well as being the 'Training Garrison' it had the Salvation Army's largest auditorium in the United Kingdom. It was the centre for many historic events. It is recorded that over one hundred and fifty thousand people visited the hall to pay their last respects at the lying in state of the founder William Booth.

The Bath stone neoclassical portico and colonnade was very impressive and when occasions on a national scale and international level were taking place it was a wonderful sight. The huge banners being held high in front of the brass bands were quite something to see.

The building survived the Blitz of the Second World War but much of the road in which it is situated was bombed. It is a very short road and as one looks down it one is faced by the huge portico of the hall at the far end. The siting of the hall was perfect for full effect on grand occasions.

After the Second World War fewer and fewer Salvation Army activities took place there and by 1970 these had ceased completely. The building was bought by the local authority and was intended for the establishment of a large comprehensive school on the site.

However, the building did not meet the educational requirements of the time and by the late 1970s part had been pulled down to make room for a new gymnasium and playground area for the existing Clapton School and by 1978 most of the Clapton Congress Hall was demolished leaving only the imposing portico and colonnade.

So, despite its listed status, this very important building has disappeared.

As children, my friends and I regularly had our games in the street interrupted by the Salvation Army brass band, usually on a Sunday afternoon. The band, with other Salvationists, would arrive and begin to play. From the house, my mother would appear and the fun would immediately cease while the music and hymn singing were in progress.

Some might say that we should not have been playing in the street on a Sunday. Maybe such persons are correct in their views, but I believe life should be a compromise and our parents were right in allowing us to play and then insisting we respect the Salvationists when they arrived. And believe me, we did just that – we would stand and listen, not daring to make any noise, and I am certain we actually enjoyed it.

I still love to hear the Salvation Army band when it plays in the street on special occasions. I know not if and when they now play in the neighbourhood of the Clapton Congress Hall. I would like to think that they do. But would people stand and listen? Everyone seems to be so intolerant of anything which interferes with their rushing hither and thither.

It seems the Clapton Congress Hall is still giving out a message. In 1999 Salvationists were interested to learn that the only remains of the building – the portico and colonnade – were now bearing a huge neon sign declaring 'EVERYTHING IS GOING TO BE ALRIGHT'. The sign was a piece of artwork commissioned from artist Martin Creed (who, in 2001, won the Turner Prize for modern art) as part of Clapton School and Groundwork Hackney's portico project.

At the very beginning of my narrative I talked of the death of my paternal grandfather and the difficulties endured by his widow and seven children. However, with good, helpful neighbours and family support, this lady and her children got through the worrying times. Set a good example by their mother, the children were all industrious. Not only did they all settle to steady work but, being very resourceful, they also made good use of their leisure time. I will write of my father and his hobbies later but I must mention his youngest brother.

At the present time when we are swamped with laid-on entertainment, radio, cinema, recorded music and television, to name only a few, it is not easy to imagine how few organised leisure activities were around at that time.

My father's young brother wanted to learn to play the trumpet. To take trumpet lessons was, I can only imagine, completely out of the question. What did he do? He joined the Salvation Army band. Photographs show clearly how proud he was of his uniform and his trumpet, albeit other photographs show his older brothers wearing his Salvation Army hat, which they had surreptitiously taken and put on in order to tease him.

The trumpet-playing stood him in good stead for the whole of his life. He played in dance bands and music filled his leisure hours. During the Second World War he was abroad with ENSA entertaining the troops, still playing his trumpet.

When the war was over he returned to his work in the leather trade, continuing his leisure activity of playing the trumpet. It was very convenient to have him to call on when a dance band was required. He and his band played the music for the dance in the evening on the day I was married, and for my brother's wedding too.

And so he continued. He never stopped. Actually he expanded his interest in the music and also played the drums in later life.

At the time of his death he was still a member of a band. He died in his sleep not long before Christmas at seventy-five years of age, and his engagements diary recorded the dates for his forthcoming Christmas engagements. What a useful member of society – successful at his work, head of a happy family and provider of a lot of enjoyment for count-less people.

3

I Want to Go Home

My mother left school at fourteen years of age, the normal school-leaving age at that time. It was all rather convenient because her birthday was just at the end of the school year.

The week before her fourteenth birthday she was taken to a local firm which produced fancy cardboard boxes, among other products made from cardboard.

It was a large, prosperous business, owned by two partners, one of whom died quite early on and the business, although it traded under its original name, was actually owned and run by the other partner and his three sons. The sons were of my parents' generation and we knew them all very well.

Everything was run in a very orderly fashion in those days, and my mother and her mother were interviewed by the boss for only a few minutes before he called in a lady who was in charge of one floor of this large firm.

There was not a great deal to discuss. My mother was asked whether she wanted to begin work by learning the fancy box-making trade, which meant, like all trades, learning the basic procedures first and then progressing to the more intricate work, or would she prefer to go to the department where she would work on various machines and of course the finished product would be mass produced?

The remuneration for the first option was ten shillings

per week, the remuneration for the second twelve shillings and sixpence per week.

Although my mother was asked which she preferred, it was her mother who answered for her. 'She will start for twelve and six, please,' she said, and my mother regretted that decision all of her life.

The lady conducting the interview recited all the rules and regulations, informed my mother at what time to arrive on the Monday morning and finally told her to bring a nice pinafore with her. She added that she never wanted to see her with a 'grubby' pinafore. 'If it gets grubby, then you take it home and come with a nice clean one the next morning.'

To be fair to my grandmother, she was not as mercenary as this episode suggests. My mother told me that she, like her brothers and sisters, was taken to the local haberdashers and provided with a complete wardrobe, including underwear, hosiery and shoes before she began working for a living. She was then given the choice of having four shillings a week returned to her for pocket money and her mother would continue to buy her clothes, or she could have six shillings back from her wages each week and buy her own clothes.

She decided to take the second option, working on the assumption that it would be some time before she needed to buy new clothes.

Manufacturing industries are renowned for having periods of high activity when their goods are in great demand, followed by what is known as 'short time', when, as the term suggests, their goods are not in such great demand and working hours are necessarily shorter.

I am told that in the box-making trade, the weeks following Christmas were the 'short time' period. Before Christmas was the very busy time with the demand for boxes to contain chocolates, cosmetics and other luxury goods.

My mother was warned by her mother never to say that she was unable to contribute to the family income because she was on 'short time'. She obviously never heeded the warning because she related to me that one Friday she arrived home from work and announced that her wages were going to be much depleted owing to 'short time' looming on the horizon. She was reminded that she could make up for the short-fall by using some of the money she had earned in the period before Christmas when she had been on 'overtime'.

My mother continued to work for the same organisation until she was expecting me. It was a very happy time, according to her. She would always remind me that it was so because 'everyone knew their place'. When the boss's sons eventually came into the business they were about the same age as my parents, but until my father retired at sixty years of age he always addressed them in a very formal manner – that was the way it was in those days and it worked very well.

My mother recalled that when both she and one of the bosses were around twenty years of age, she undid her pinafore, anticipating the bell to announce the end of the working day. Just at that moment the young boss walked past, noticed her pinafore and without stopping said, 'Do up your pinny, Catherine. The bell hasn't gone yet.'

'But,' my mother added, 'I saw him smiling to himself as he went out of the door.' And she was not in the least offended by his remark.

The company's premises were only two hundred yards from my home and it was always referred to as 'the firm'. The management's dealings with the workforce were strict but friendly and understanding. Many of the employees worked there for a long time.

*

38

When he left school my father continued to work with horses, as he had been doing in his spare time. But after a year he decided to settle to something more permanent. He began work in 'the firm' a few months after my mother.

It must have been an attraction of opposites. He was a quiet, thoughtful fellow, while my mother was quick-tempered, lively and always giggling – so I am told. He was as dark-eyed and dark-haired as she was fair. One day when I was a teenager, I was walking with my mother when we met the lady who had conducted the original interview with my mother when she applied for her job. She informed me that she had thought, when she first saw my mother, that she had only just begun to live in London because, 'with her long hair the colour of corn and her rosy-apple cheeks she looked like a country lass'.

So began a long courtship, not unusual in those days. After three years they were engaged and following a two-year engagement they were married.

Everything followed a set pattern. Although they would, like most other couples, begin married life in just two or three rooms, probably upstairs in a relative's house, these rooms would be furnished down to the last small detail. My mother, like all efficient 'wives to be', had her bottom drawer. In her case it was a five-foot long chest in which she stored all her carefully chosen household linen, blankets, towels etc., in readiness for the wedding. I remember that chest well.

On Saturday evenings my parents, with my father's brother and his fiancée, would regularly visit a warehouse to view and decide which articles of furniture and household necessities they would eventually buy when they had saved enough money.

Apparently, they derived great pleasure from this. No rushing into marriage up to their eyes in debt for them. They planned everything in great detail and it seems to have paid dividends, and in fact most of the marriages at that time appear to have been successful.

They would relate to me little stories of what happened when they bought certain items. For instance, we had a sideboard in our home of which I was very fond. It had pillars supporting a high top and the back of this sideboard was a huge mirror. The story was that a local furniture-maker had been keeping this particular timber for a long time. He was going to make the sideboard as a silver-wedding gift for his wife. Unfortunately, he began gambling on horses and needed ready cash, enabling my parents to buy the sideboard for their future home.

I mentioned earlier that my father and his brothers made good use of their leisure time. My father was quite artistic, and this aptitude influenced the work which he settled to for the rest of his working life.

When asked what he did for a living, he would always describe himself as a printer. He was actually the composi-tor in 'the firm'. As a child, I loved to visit his little domain in the factory. It was all so interesting. He not only set up the type, as the term compositor suggests, he also designed the boxes and then designed the decoration for the outside of the boxes appropriately for whatever was to be their content, be it perfume, chocolates or whatever. It was an intricate procedure. He would then set up the printing blocks, filling in the spaces between type and decoration with little blocks of wood. It fascinated me to watch him at work.

If ever we had a box to be disposed of which he con-sidered to be unusual in some way, he would painstakingly undo it until it was completely flat. I think it was just out of interest. He also enjoyed drawing and painting, and I can remember from when I was a small child he would explain to me the mixing of paints and all about prime colours. He was not terribly proficient at painting pictures, but when he eventually moved out of London at seventy-four years of age he was still attending evening classes in art.

My father's other leisure activity, apart from gardening – all three surviving brothers were very keen gardeners – was sport.

He became very interested in the art of boxing after joining the Eton Manor Club at about fifteen years of age.

The origin of the club was way back in about 1880 when the urban population was increasing rapidly and, without welfare benefits as we know them, poverty was very much in evidence. While there were politicians looking to government to represent the poor and unemployed, there were other wealthy persons who too had come to the conclusion that something would have to be done.

Eton College did more than consider the necessary social changes – they did something practical about it. It was decreed by the college authorities that all their scholars should contribute a regular amount to be put in trust and used for the people of Hackney Wick, particularly the young.

Very soon a mission church was established and many of the Eton scholars who had gone on to university eventually went to live at this mission and devoted their lives to the welfare of the local people. One of these was Gerald Valerian Wellesley of the great Wellington family, who arrived in Hackney Wick in 1907. My father often spoke of him, saying that he had the ability to speak to and endear himself to all members of society and was never patronising.

Although a boys' club had been established at the mission, Mr Wellesley wanted to establish a boys' club independent of the church. Bigger premises were found

41

and, what is more important, he was joined in his venture by other Old Etonians who, with their specialised knowledge, particularly in the all-important world of finance, made it possible for the Eton Manor Club to progress in the best possible ways.

There were four original trustees and well before the First World War they envisaged new and bigger premises. The new magnificent spacious building designed by an Old Etonian was completed in 1913 and opened by General Lord Roberts. The design incorporated a large central hall equipped with a stage. This was used regularly as a gymnasium, for general training and boxing training and tournaments, and was also a venue for dances, concerts and stage shows. I remember seeing their stage shows. They were hilarious – all the more so because all the participants were male.

At ground level in the central building was a non-alcoholic bar and at the rear were wonderful bathrooms and showers. Those wonderful Etonian trustees had soon realised that most of the club members lived in houses without bathrooms.

The boys were eligible to join the club at thirteen years ten months, but were only on probation. 'Subs' were an infinitesimal sum. Soon other Old Etonians, after completing their studies at university, would join the trustees, bringing various talents with them, not only sports, often at international level, but also dramatics, art, music etc.

At the back of the club was a delightful old manor house where Arthur Villiers, another of the trustees, lived. As a child I was acquainted with this gentleman simply because he lived on the premises and was therefore more in evidence than other trustees. But there were other gentlemen who did great things for the club.

Two of the other gentlemen who managed the club had played rugby football for Oxford University and London clubs. They introduced the game to the club at a time when the young men of Hackney Wick described it as 'toffee-nosed' and 'upstage'. But it did not take these young men long to learn the rules of the game and how to handle the peculiarly elongated ball.

I can only hope it doesn't sound too patronising to record that the trustees and managers brought to the club the best of public school spirit – to play fiercely but honourably, to give no quarter and expect none and to be courteous to the opposition. These gentlemen with their connections were able to build a fixture list with some of the best clubs – even organising an annual match with Eton College.

Early in the 1920s the trustees acquired about two hundred acres of land on Hackney Marshes, which became known as the Wilderness. The Wilderness was made into one of the finest sports grounds in the country. At one time the club was turning out fifteen soccer teams, and the rugby section had a superb pitch.

That was the formal history of the club, but from a personal angle it coloured my whole childhood and teenage years, and for my father it is no exaggeration to say his family and the club were his life.

They had a publication which was produced regularly, maybe once a month, maybe not so frequently, called the *Chin-wag*. My father collected these for years and I can remember, when at teacher training college, going through these publications when working on a project about leisure time and pursuits. Reading them so fascinated me it was a miracle that I found time to complete the assignment.

Until he died, my father always wore the club's badge on his blazer pocket and it was also attached to the front of his car.

After joining the club, he soon became interested in boxing and that remained his main interest. As a youth, he took part in amateur boxing contests and won many trophies and medals. I always liked the story of the evening he had won a rather important medal and met my mother after the contest. As she and I walked along she would point to the exact spot where he had shown her this medal. It was just under the railway bridge because that was where there was a street-light.

As he became too old to take part in boxing tournaments, he became the trainer for the club and managed all the boxing activities.

I always spent a great deal of my time with him and I would accompany him when there were boxing tournaments at the club or elsewhere. I have a recollection of attending the Amateur Boxing Championships the very evening when I should have been revising for one of my School Certificate Examinations.

Very little stopped my father from his regular trips to the Eton Manor Club. If he had a head cold and was 'suffering', my mother would tell us not to worry. 'He thinks it's pneumonia but he will have recovered by Friday.' Which he always did, in time to go training.

During the Second World War he was deferred by his firm from service in the armed forces but he became the physical training instructor in the local Air Training Corps. I often accompanied him if they were meeting on a Saturday afternoon, probably for a boxing tournament, and would assist the officer's wife by helping with the refreshments.

From a very young age, I would go with him on the long walk to the Wilderness, where there was always something interesting going on. I would watch men playing 'tennis', not against each other but against a wall. It intrigued me, but I never questioned it and it was about thirty years later before I realised the game was squash.

All kinds of events were celebrated at the club and one that stands out in my memory was held at the Wilderness. It may have been the Silver Jubilee of King George V or the Coronation of King George VI. I would have been six years of age if the first and eight years of age if the second. Not very old, but I can recall many events that day.

There were competitions for every sport one can imagine. The Dagenham Girl Pipers gave a wonderful display. But the grand finale was outstanding when one considers how long ago it took place. All day they had been filming events as they happened, and at the end of the evening the film was shown on a huge open-air screen. This was followed by the most spectacular firework display, which included a huge firework picture of the King and Queen.

How I wish I had not disposed of the hoard of *Chin-wag* magazines. They contained so much interesting information about the club, which turned out national- and inter-national-class performers at every sport. They excelled at boxing, and two brothers won Amateur Boxing Association and Olympic Championships.

I was and still am amazed that anyone could possibly disapprove of such an institution, but that was the case when I submitted my project at college. I remember clearly that although I was given a good mark for it, the lecturer referred to it as 'paternalistic'. It was always my opinion that he was just envious that certain well-meaning persons could actually afford to do something beneficial for their fellow men,.

My mother should also be given some credit for the part she played. For some years immediately following the Second World War she practically had 'open-house' for a particular group of club boxers. They would arrive in the evening and she would supply endless cups of tea. Saturday was obviously their favourite time. My father had a set of drums, I would play the piano and we would all spend hours just chatting and singing. It all sounds so boring now, there was no alcohol – all the boys were usually in training. My mother would make tea and sandwiches continually. I often wonder how she managed it with such strict rationing at that time.

It was all such innocent, good fun. No alcohol, therefore no-one ever became drunk. Gradually girlfriends appeared, they too would visit my home and became friends of the family. One by one they married, and eventually those particular boys gave up boxing but continued to spend time at the club, and my father continued with his interest in the boxing scene.

Towards the end of the Second World War it was suggested that a club for girls be set up. Until that time girls were in no way connected with the club, except as spectators at sports events or in attendance at social functions.

The girls' club was only very small in numbers – no more than a handful to begin with. We were given premises, not in the boys' premises, but adequate for our needs. It gradually grew but I do not think there were ever more than fifty at any one time, perhaps even less.

But it was a super little club. We were shifted to larger premises and had a lady who made our evening refreshments. No males were ever to be seen, with the exception of one of the boys' PT instructors, who visited our club every Friday evening to put us through our paces. Also their swimming coach, who would meet us at the local swimming baths once a week in the evening and try to improve our swimming abilities.

There was one concession given to the girls' club in regard to the Eton Manor Club's sports facilities. They had a netball pitch marked out for us and we regularly used it on Sunday afternoons when practising for matches, which were played on Saturdays.

It goes without saying that the pitch was in the Wilderness grounds, but still there was no socialising with the male club members. However, there was one exception to this rule. If we were ever short to make up our teams during netball

46

practice, we would ask the rugby players, who were always around, if one of their number would help us out. There was one rugby player – he was either the brother or boyfriend of one of our members – who was always willing to come to our aid. A huge, gentle giant whom we would put in the position of 'defence', thereby making the end result of the game a foregone conclusion.

I married and moved away, but a group of our club members continued to meet in each other's homes and, fifty years on are still good friends and continue meeting.

In the 1960s the London County Council informed Arthur Villiers that a new road system out of London would mean the demolition of the club buildings. He was offered an alternative site but decided to close the club for good. Social changes may have influenced his decision. Boys were not using the club as much as in the past and the upkeep of the club buildings and all the Wilderness facilities was hardly justified.

So, the club was demolished. I often visit that area of London and as I drive on to the dual carriageway leading to the Blackwall Tunnel on my way home to Kent, I pass the spot where the club building once stood and I always feel terribly, terribly sad that such a wonderful institution has disappeared.

The Wilderness was turned over to the Lea Valley Authority. But some sections, the rugby in particular, fought valiantly to survive and are still around in new surroundings.

My father's time at the Eton Manor Club must have been during the club's heyday. Mum and Dad would both reminisce about it. But they appeared also to have enjoyed their working day together. He would accompany my mother at lunch-time to her home, where her mother would supply the lunch. She was a superb cook. This little ritual continued

47

after they were married, although they set up home upstairs in my father's family house.

This was the usual practice at that time. By the time my father married there were only two younger siblings living at home with their mother, and therefore two of the upstairs rooms were vacant. My parents settled in there, utilising the landing for a small kitchen area. This too was the usual practice, not only in those times but until many, many years later. The design of the houses made this possible.

But the house, like so many thousands, had no water upstairs. It is difficult to imagine how exhausting life must be if one needs to carry up the stairs every drop of water required for cooking, washing up, cleaning etc. Fortunately, in my mother's situation the wash-house was perfect for the laundry work. Not all families living in these circumstances had this facility.

I try to imagine, but find it impossible to do so, how much water would have been required in one day. Just to rinse the vegetables for a meal, the water would need to be taken up and then taken down again. How many times in a day do we turn on the tap in the kitchen?

I find it utterly incomprehensible, but it was quite acceptable then. My mother coped with the situation for the first ten years of her married life, by which time I was eight and my brother three years old. And that just opens up a whole new train of thought – nappies – the rinsing of – the washing of – the boiling of – when the babies arrived on the scene.

But somehow my parents and so many others succeeded in creating a happy, beautiful, comfortable environment.

This was brought home to me one day when I was shopping with my mother. Quite often when we were out together my mother would recognise a lady who, she would explain to me, was the health visitor at the time she was expecting me.

By the time I was in my late teens, instead of just giving

48

the customary nod to each other, my mother and the lady would have a little chat. The health visitor had retired and had time to stop.

This particular day she was very communicative and set about imparting information to me in a very earnest way. In retrospect, was she giving me a little lecture and guidance? She told me that my mother made preparations for my arrival that were 'worthy of a princess'. These were her actual words to me. I was also told that Mum's home was so cosy that she, the health visitor, would call in for a cup of tea although her work did not necessitate this. 'She kept it like a little palace.' Once again, these were her actual words to me.

This acquaintanceship had continued for a few years, and the same health visitor was on the scene when my brother was expected five years later. So, she had seen Mum in her role as a mother also, and she praised her highly, saying that her good, sound common sense when dealing with babies and young children was as good as any psychologist's.

I like to think that I had gleaned a little of her expertise when dealing with my own toddlers, but I know that I was not as proficient as she. I remember not taking her good advice on a few occasions and am aware that I was in error.

Mum, like her mother before her was very strict but so very, very kind. Well into her eighties she would keep bars of chocolate to hand, ready to give to the children who lived next door to her. As they went by her window she would dart up and out, to call them and give them their little treat.

I was the first grandchild to arrive on the scene on my mother's side of the family. As often happens, I was swiftly followed by first one cousin and then another until there were a few of us. My mother, her sisters and her sister-in-

49

law would spend many afternoons in my grandmother's house and garden with their children. They all lived locally and this appeared to be their favourite venue.

My grandmother was not always present on these occasions. She was a real film buff and would often take herself off to the cinema, particularly if Clark Gable or George Raft were on screen. Oh how she adored Clark Gable! And it made her afternoon complete if she could return home, having had a good cry, to find a lovely fresh pastry reserved for her.

While she was at the cinema a member of the family would be dispatched to the local bakery to purchase wonderful fresh-baked pastries to accompany their endless cups of tea and chat. And we were all aware that a pastry must be put aside for Nanny. I think these afternoons were a very wise move on the part of my grandmother, resulting in a few hours of peace away from the hubbub which ensued back home once the ladies and children arrived.

But all good things come to an end and the time arrived for me to begin school. Five years was the age by which all children had to commence this new adventure, but starting at a younger age was quite usual. It is interesting to note that many schools now take the children before they are five years of age, whereas this was not so for many years. When I was teaching, if the child had not reached five years of age by the beginning of the term, they quite often had to wait until the next term.

At the time when my education began, I remember, although the school was surrounded by a high brick wall, through the gates one could see the long row of camp beds in the playground placed adjacent to the school building. The small children always had an afternoon sleep, and in the warm weather this took place in the open air.

I was four years and three months old when it was decided I should start school. I insisted that I take my quite large, fancy cardboard box with me. My father had given it to me, and it was decorated with a large ribbon bow. Obviously a box which I carried around as a comforter, it had probably been discarded at his place of work. My own children never had any such item that I can recall, but two or three of the grandchildren did have various objects to which they were very attached and from which they derived great comfort. I have a school group photograph, taken when I was five years of age, and I am standing with the box securely tucked under my arm.

The first day of term I was deposited at school and my mother, like so many other mothers, was probably reluctant to leave. In my teaching career when a child was arriving for the first time I would often have to be very insistent that Mum leave and allow me to cope with the unhappy child.

But my mother, being a very sensible lady, did leave, and maybe I would have settled if the weather had not been so nice as to permit the opening of the classroom door to the playground. A gate was always secured across the bottom half of the opening to prevent children 'escaping', but as my mother walked home, she heard two other mothers commenting on the little girl with the box who was trying to get out by climbing up the gate like a little monkey and screaming, 'I want to go home.'

This continued for a few days until it was suggested my school debut be postponed until I reached five years of age.

During the few days I attended school I managed to catch measles. I was very ill, so I am told. This was the only time my health gave cause for concern as a child. Although small, I was always quite fit. But having measles and needing to recuperate was the final determinant in deciding to keep me at home until I was five.

The following year I returned to school and loved it from the first day. I was very fortunate in that I had always spent a lot of time with my father, who would encourage me in

51

every way, and this I am sure gave me the confidence which I as a teacher know to be so important for a child's progress.

The first Christmas a play was enacted by the infants. The setting was a toyshop, and I was to be the fairy doll in a box. The headmistress was also taking part and she had to remove me from the box, sit me on her lap and wind me up so that I could move around.

I remember clearly watching my father making my wings and covering my slippers with glue to enable him to sprinkle them with silver glitter. The wand had the same treatment. After the performance I went with my parents to have my photograph taken. I still have it.

I am aware that I appear to have been spoiled but I prefer to believe that I was just advantageously encouraged. In complete contrast to this wimpish child who gives the impression of a baby always 'wanting to go home', it seems I was always willing to 'have a go' at anything.

The school I attended had three floors, like so many others, particularly in London. They are still to be seen as one drives around. The three floors catered for the pupils from the commencement of their time at school to the age of fourteen, when they were required to leave.

On the ground floor were the infants' classes, consisting of both boys and girls. But on reaching seven years of age we girls remained in the building to join the junior and then senior school and were joined by the girls from another local school. Our boys at seven went off to the other school to unite with their boys. Therefore after the age of seven the schools were single-sex. Never have I been taught by a male teacher. I can only write of the schools of my knowledge but I assume that the procedure was similar or the same in most schools which came under the London County Council Authority.

Many people are of the opinion that mixed-sex schools and being taught by a member of the opposite sex is advantageous to the social development of young persons. My only response is that my generation never had any problems socialising with the opposite sex during or after our years spent in education.

Before the 1944 Education Act all children were entitled to an elementary school education which terminated at fourteen years of age, unless parents were prepared to pay for secondary education for the children at the age of eleven or the junior school pupil was awarded a Junior County Scholarship to secondary education. At that time there were also junior technical schools and technical colleges for pupils who possessed the skills required by these establishments.

My parents were summoned to the school when I was six years old and told that the school had hopes of my becoming a 'scholarship girl'. Instead of waiting until I reached seven years of age, it was suggested I become a junior at the age of six. But it seems there was a problem. The middle floor of the school was at that time being used by another school (I know not why) and it was necessary that we climb the stairs to the top floor. Because I was only just six years of age and also rather small, my parents' permission was sought.

Naturally permission was given. I am quite certain that my father would have carried me up and down rather than discourage any educational advantage which I was being offered.

But once up on the top floor of the building, there was no necessity for descending and ascending during the school day because our playground and toilets were on the roof of the school. Safety was paramount, not only was the roof surrounded by a high wall but on top of this was high wire mesh. The school bell was also on the roof and, believe me, it was extremely loud if you happened to be up there when it rang, as it did every day.

4

I Did Not Want to Go Home

I have already given a brief description of my maternal grandmother's house but I think it deserves a more detailed elucidation. It was a wonderful venue for numerous activities.

The stables at the far end of the garden were rented out after my grandmother moved her wood-chopping business to another site. The stable on the left housed the huge horse and cart belonging to the greengrocer who had a permanent stall in the local market. The horse was big and gentle, with huge feet. The size of his hooves fascinated me, they were so large.

When trading in the market ceased for the day the greengrocer would load up his cart and return to the stable. It was always a treat if we just 'happened' to be visiting Big Nanny at that time. She would open the gates in readiness for his return, then he would lead the horse as it pulled the cart through the covered entrance and the garden to the stable. We loved to hear the clip-clop of his hooves as it echoed on his way through.

Once in the stable, the greengrocer would set about settling the horse for the night. We were allowed to watch this procedure from a safe distance. First the horse was unhitched from the cart and then his harness was removed, which always seemed rather a complex practice. The horse was fed and watered and given a rub down. After it was made comfortable its owner would sit on a bale of straw in the corner of the stable and clean and polish the various parts of the harness.

I am aware that my cousins and I were extremely fortunate in that we were able to witness such a routine quite regularly, living as we were not in a rural setting but in a densely inhabited area of London where such opportunities were rare.

The second stable, the one on the right, was rented by a chimney-sweep. Unlike the presence of the greengrocer's horse and cart which in every respect was only a source of joy and happiness, the presence of the chimney-sweep's handcart was quite often a problem to our mothers and a source of unhappiness to the younger generation.

When he returned from his day's labour the chimney-sweep would push his cart through to the stable and proceed to set the tools of his trade in order, preparing for the following day's work. Unfortunately, this was in the days before vacuum chimney sweeping. It was at the time when the sweep would push the brush up the chimney and continue to lengthen this until the brush showed at the top of the chimney, but instead of the soot being sucked up by a vacuum cleaner as now happens, the soot when dislodged would all fall into the grate and have to be swept up and put into bags, to be taken away by the sweep. Any children in the house would stand in the garden waiting for the brush to appear above the chimney and rush in to inform the sweep when it did so.

It was this soot and these sooty brushes and rods which the said chimney-sweep brought back to the stable.

It was not the fault of the sweep that we nosey children sometimes found his cart and apparatus temptingly interesting. Children like to investigate anything unusual and we often did so, knowing probably full well what the result would be. It always was surprising how much mess just a minuscule amount of soot could make. Smudges of soot would appear everywhere – on clothes, hands and faces.

Usually we children were taken home before the sweep returned from work (very wise), but I was in trouble on more than one occasion because my parents and I lived with my grandparents for a short time (more of that later) and I was on hand to investigate alone, and I did just that.

Fortunately, Auntie Nellie had returned home from work by the time the sweep left and was able to save me from the worst of my mother's wrath. She was a young lady by this time and engaged to be married. She still adores all children and was then looking forward to being married and raising a family of her own. But life can be so unfair and cruel. She had three babies who all died before the age of six months.

I commented earlier on the very quick tempers possessed by my mother and her siblings. Auntie Nellie, who is and always was a very calm and gentle person, was the refuge for my cousins and me when we were being scolded on many occasions.

She still remembers vividly being so concerned when I was being well and truly remonstrated with by my mother that she scooped me up in her arms and ran off with me until my mother had calmed down.

I had spoiled my clothes and my person, I imagine, with the soot once again. My mother's reaction I find quite understandable. I was always very well dressed. My outdoor clothes were made by a tailor and other items of clothing were made by a local dressmaker. I would like to emphasise the point that although this sounds very grand it was a quite usual practice at that time.

It was a time when young people would leave school at fourteen and learn their trade thoroughly, be it tailoring or dressmaking. They did not need to be given a pattern, but just took one's measurements and asked for a description of one's requirements.

I would be taken to a tailoring establishment and I can remember standing on a table in the middle of a room to be measured, while the machinists were sitting at their sewing machines and other ladies were sewing by hand in the room.

It was only in the last three or four decades of the twentieth century that this practice appears to have become virtually non-existent.

I remember having a coat and hat made for me when I was about six years of age. It was made from hunting pink, the cloth used by foxhunters for their jackets. It had a black velvet collar and belted back with black velvet buttons from top to bottom. It had rather a full skirt, pleated at the back. When I had outgrown the coat, the lady who owned the local haberdashery shop wanted it so that she might take it to pieces to enable her to make a pattern from it. She was a dressmaker and a very good friend of my mother. But my mother decided to give the coat to a lady who had always admired it. This lady had quite a large family and it fitted one of her daughters.

Back to Mum's family. When my mother's elder brother returned home after World War I his leg was permanently disabled and he was unable to return to the work at which he was employed before the war.

After being hospitalised a number of times for operations on his leg, he eventually began to seek permanent employment. He had been left with one leg shorter than the other and was convinced that wearing the shoes which were offered him, one shoe being built up on the outside to make up the difference in leg length, would be a drawback. So, he had shoes made, one of which was built up on the inside. My mother told me that it was remarkable the difference this made to his self-confidence and he found a new career as a commercial traveller.

Auntie Nellie tells me what a tall, blond and handsome man he was. He was in his twenties and very popular. In the areas to which his work necessitated regular visits, he got into a routine of lodging at the same establishment on every trip. Even now Auntie Nellie reminisces about how she would look forward to his returning home from these periods away from home.

In June 1932 there must have been at least one lovely warm balmy evening, because on such evenings my grandmother and grandfather and perhaps other family members would open the big gates of the side entrance and sit just inside and relax, chatting to neighbours who were passing by.

On one of these evenings they were surprised to see a policeman walking towards them. He was obviously looking for a particular house, carefully noting the number on each door as he progressed along the road until he reached the small group enjoying their evening relaxation. He did not ask if they resided at the number he was seeking, perhaps uncertain as they were not directly outside the house but seated just inside the wide side entrance. Instead he established my grandmother's name, which by then had been the surname of her second husband for many years.

The young policeman then asked if they knew of a family living in the road with a certain surname. They directed the policeman to a house further down the road, as it did not register with my grandmother that the name he was seeking was the same as hers from her first marriage.

The policeman thanked her for her help, but unfortunately added without any warning, for which on his part there was no necessity under the circumstances, that he was pleased for her sake that his official business was not with her, as he was the bearer of bad news. He had to inform the other lady that her son William was dead.

One can imagine my grandmother's reaction to this news. There had been no preparation or sympathetic build-up to this statement. She immediately put together the two names and realised her son William was the person to whom the policeman was referring.

The young policeman, who I was told was very young and probably inexperienced at this kind of undertaking, was extremely upset for what had occurred.

We often hear people refer to the 'bad old days', while others bring to mind the 'good old days'. I think it would be more appropriate to think of earlier times as just the days when the lot of society was gradually being improved, culminating in the materialisation of our Welfare State.

The powers that be were not heartless on all occasions, and this sad family event and the reaction it produced were a good example of this. An organisation, I know not which, only that it was connected to my uncle's service in the army and his subsequent injuries, offered to bring home his body.

Although most of society must surely be considered at the very least marginally better off financially now than then, there are many who would still gratefully accept this offer. Not my grandmother, independent as always, she travelled with her younger son up to Wolverhampton, collected the body and accompanied it on its journey home. He was laid to rest with his photograph set in the headstone in Manor Park Cemetery in London.

When my grandmother visited the house where her son had stayed regularly in Wolverhampton and where he was found dead in bed, she became easier in her mind.

Once again, it has to be imagined the difficulties with which she had to cope. There was no private car available to her, just public transport. She had to arrange for the transporting of the body, the funeral in London and the official business which always accompanies the finding of a body when a person has died in their sleep. She also had to collect his personal effects.

My mother told me that her mother had always fretted about where he stayed on his various business trips, but when she met the landlady in whose house he had died her mind was put at rest. The landlady was a motherly type who clearly loved having my uncle in the house and told my grandmother that he had been like a son to her. She said that he had returned the night before feeling extremely tired and, due to the fact that he would not be working the next day, he requested that she let him sleep in the next morning and not bring his usual cup of tea to rouse him. Consequently, she did not find him until mid-morning, when she had begun to be a little concerned. He had died of a heart attack while sleeping.

It was a very sad time, not only for my grandmother but for the whole family as he was a great favourite. My father, who was one of his three brothers-in-law, used to tell me, 'He was a great chap.'

The family was expanding quite rapidly. Three of the daughters were married and the remaining son also. There were by now three grandchildren too. A good example of the 'extended family' was taking shape.

Not only were the afternoon meetings of the mothers and children still taking place but the fathers too had their recreation time catered for.

I explained in great detail the lay-out and use of the stables at the rear of my grandmother's garden, but there were other bits of the property which were put to good use also. The huge side entrance, which was part of the building and therefore under cover, but open at the rear, was used for various activities. The men had a snooker table there and would spend hours displaying their expertise.

After their tea, cakes and gossip sessions in the afternoons the ladies would go home, have their evening meals with their husbands and then all would return for a social evening. The children would play in the garden and probably get in the way of the snooker players.

One evening when we arrived we heard music and to our (the children's) delight there in the side entrance was a barrel organ. During the day a gentleman had arrived at the house and asked permission to deposit the barrel organ on my grandmother's premises. He was in the area to play the organ at a local fête and someone had suggested that my grandmother might take care of it for a couple of nights. It is easily imagined the fun we had playing it that evening. The children had never seen or heard anything like it before and in all probability never since. My grandmother's protestations went unheeded and we all had a wonderful time.

There were only ten houses in the street in which I lived, too few to warrant street parties for special occasions, so as usual we would all meet at Big Nanny's and join in the fun of her road.

The Silver Jubilee in 1935 of King George V and also the coronation in 1937 of King George VI were celebrated by street parties, and long tables were erected under cover on Big Nanny's premises to leave the street clear for the party activities. Children remember such events and in view of the wonderful celebrations which took place recently to celebrate Queen Elizabeth II's Golden Jubilee, many children will have cause to remember that day as I had cause to remember her father's coronation.

For one reason or another that side entrance on grandmother's property was put to good use. So too was the upper portion of her outbuildings at the rear. As I have mentioned, between the two stables was a large area open at the front, and situated at the back of this space against the wall was a staircase leading to 'the loft'. And believe me this loft was a hive of activity. About two-thirds of it was used by the men, mostly for carpentry or any other what we now call 'do-it-yourself' activities. There was always a lovely smell of new timber. I remember my father made a dining table which had large elaborately carved legs. He also made my parents' wardrobe.

Now that so many children are brought up in the nuclear type of family they miss a lot of the conviviality of the extended family. The playgroups and mother-and-toddler groups are in plentiful supply, doing their best to give children the opportunities they need to socialise. But it is my opinion they do not fully take the place of the extended family meetings where all generations from great-grand-parents to small children can spend time together. It is not the fault or the wish of the parents, but the problem so often now is that everyone is more mobile, which in itself is a necessity when seeking employment. Many more young persons go on to further education, and once they have left the family home so often they do not return to it, or to the area where they grow up.

Until the outbreak of World War II, many of my evenings and weekends were spent with my extended family at Big Nanny's, but I believe the happiest times for me were when I would accompany my father either to the sports ground of his club – or to the loft at Big Nanny's, for the simple reason that Aladdin's Cave for me was the opposite end of the carpentry area, because there my father had his printing press. I cannot begin to describe the sheer joy I got from watching him at work.

The printing press was a huge black free-standing appa-ratus. To one my size, it resembled a large monster, particularly when my father had it going. It was worked by hand and I would watch while he pulled down a lever of some kind to complete each operation. Each of these was accompanied by a loud clunk. But it was not a frightening sound to me; I enjoyed every clunk and marvelled at the results. I still can hear that sound and smell the ink and paper.

Carrying on the family tradition of resourcefulness, my father had a work area in the loft which resembled his place of work. But as well as preparing the work for printing as in his place of employment, he also completed the work on his own printing press in the loft.

Whereas his regular daily work entailed designing boxes in detail and designing the wording and decoration to go on these boxes for large well-known companies, be they chocolate manufacturers, cosmetic firms or whatever, the customers for his small business were the local tradespeople and shopkeepers.

Most of his work involved the printing of advertising material for these small businesses, and anything else which required the setting up, design and duplicating process.

This was before the advent of the plastic bag, when most items when purchased would be put in a paper bag. Now, the name of the shop is seen on the plastic bag but then the name and/or the logo would be printed on these paper bags, and this was a large proportion of my father's work.

There were two designs which I can recall. The first was a brown paper bag – quite large – on which was printed the name of the local shoe-repairer and a lady's shoe. The second was a white bag which was used by a local dairy. The logo on this was a milk churn. The bags were used when selling dairy products in the shop, but they were also advertising the side of the business which was the daily delivery of milk.

I can remember one occurrence when my father did a great deal of work in preparation for the coronation of King

Edward VIII. My memory is of various articles being produced and decorated in red, white and blue. My father brought home some articles – I know not what they were, but remember my mother and me threading red, white and blue ribbon through the holes which had been punched out. I know he printed calendars for the following year, which was a line of the business on his own behalf, not undertaken for any other local businessman.

As we all know, that coronation did not take place, and Dad lost out financially. However, when King George VI was crowned soon after this, my father was able to recoup some of his loss with the profit from the work that this event produced.

I was able to spend a lot of time with my father because his place of employment was so close to our home, two minutes from door to door. Our main meal of the day was at lunch-time, and we had tea when my father returned from work. My earliest memories are first of myself standing at the front door or at the gate to the side entrance, waiting for my father to return home for midday dinner, running to meet him, being scooped up in his arms and given a piggyback to the house and up the stairs to our flat. Second down memory lane is one of these rather silly little happenings which seem to stay with us for ever. In this case it is remembering how, after we had eaten our meal and before my father returned to work, I would sit on his lap and we would sing a song which I believe was called, 'Dance, Dance, Dance Little Sunbeam', and at a certain word in the song I would bump his head on the wall.

I am aware of how idiotic it sounds, but nothing will shake my belief that by experiencing this rather silly little ritual day after day, I and probably many more children at that time who were able to be in the company of their parents so often, were more fortunate than so many of the under school-age children today who spend a large part of their day and eat their lunch in a nursery.

I am not deprecating day nurseries because I am aware that for financial reasons they are sometimes a necessary solution, allowing both parents to bring in an income. I am just making an observation and commenting on the fact that for a pre-school child it is not such an emotionally advantageous setting as being at home in a family environment.

When I reached school age I was allowed to spend even more time with my father. He had made up his mind to buy a house and was enthusiastically saving for the deposit. That, my mother told me, was the reason for his printing press work.

He would return from work, change his clothes, have his meal and then set off, carrying a freshly laundered overall which resembled a beige heavy linen coat with sleeves, which he wore to protect his clothes from the printing ink. He always wore one of these garments at his place of work. In point of fact he always donned this protective clothing at home when working in the garden or in his 'huts', which were two small brick buildings he had built himself and housed everything and anything which might be required for any purpose imaginable.

They were like another Aladdin's Cave to me and although I knew that I would be in trouble with my father, I could not resist going in. I would potter about, looking for suitable pieces of wood, which I would plane, nail together and paint. My favourite was always fashioning a warship, made with shaped pieces of wood one on top of the other, getting smaller as the warship got taller. The finishing touch was painting it. This was when I knew I would get a telling-off, because my father continually reprimanded me for breaking the skin which always formed on the surface of his pots of paint. But he was very patient with me and I can see him now in my mind's eye, watching me put pieces of wood in the vice to hold them still while I sawed and planed them.

If Dad was not busy in his huts, he would be working at his printing press. More often than not, after eating our meal he would set off for Big Nanny's with me in tow. I would spend an hour or two with him, during which time I would be given the task of carefully stacking the paper bags he had printed. I also had the job of counting them. Doubtless my helping was of minimal use and had to be carried out again by my father, but it helped to make a happy partnership.

Dad would take me home when it was my bedtime. As children, we had a regular time for going to bed. Perhaps because the parents spent so much of their time during the day with their offspring, they felt they were entitled to a few hours to themselves in the evening.

In my case it was also because I was an extremely bad-tempered child if I was kept up late in the evening. I am certain this was true because it has been verified by my mother, my aunts, and my grandmother, who, I am told, was always the first to suggest that I be taken home and put to bed.

And so my father would deliver me home, but his day's work was still not over. He would return to the printing press. Mum told me that it would often be midnight by the time he had delivered the printed paper bags by small hand cart (no car then) to the local shopkeepers, who also kept late hours. Small businessmen worked long and hard then, and I believe still do, to keep that feeling of independence.

My father was still saving for the deposit on a house, but by the time I was just five years of age his youngest brother had married and only his mother and youngest sister were living in the house with us, enabling my parents and me to occupy the three upstairs rooms.

66

The largest room, which was in the front of the house, was used as the bedroom, accommodating my parents' double bed and my large cot. It must have been a pretty large cot because, although quite small, I was five years old. The cot was situated with the head in the alcove beside the chimney breast, which was on the side flank wall of the house.

Structural work was being carried out at this time on the flank wall, including work on the chimney. I am told that it was quite a big undertaking, with scaffolding being used. The builders had finished work for the day and I was being prepared for bed when there was the most dreadful noise. Dreadful, I think, can hardly describe it, because the chimney had collapsed, taking the scaffolding with it – and not only the scaffolding but part of the upper flank wall too. My cot was still standing but only just. The head end was on the edge of what had been the wall. Fortunately, I was not in it.

My mother was just two months pregnant at the time, so this, coupled with my close call, obviously panicked everyone. The baker who owned the house heard the crash, rushed out to his back garden and saw the sight of his builders' scaffolding in a state of collapse.

He insisted my parents and I quickly visit the doctor's surgery which was next door but one to his shop. At that time and for many years, doctors' and dentists' surgeries were always open in the early evening to accommodate patients who were working during the day. It was the norm to visit them on one's way home from work.

I can recall the visit, as it was the only visit I paid to the doctor until my late teens. No physical harm was experienced by anyone, but the wall was in a mess. We were obliged to vacate our home and appear on Big Nanny's doorstep. She had plenty of room to accommodate us, because by this time she and Grandad also had only their youngest daughter still living at home.

I can remember having a lovely time during the few weeks we were living there, but for my mother it wasn't quite so enjoyable. Although she loved visiting her old family home at practically every opportune moment, circumstances at that time were not conducive to her well-being. I was in close proximity to the forbidden soot and she was terribly worried about their home and contents. Added to this, the effect of her pregnancy was severe morning sickness. Poor Mum. She once said to me, 'If I had known that the wall was going to fall down, your brother would have been a few months younger!'

Eventually the builders completed their work and we returned home. A few years later when my father bought the house he must have been happy knowing of the structural repairs which had already been carried out.

The next outstanding event in my life, and believe me I exaggerate not, was the birth of my brother. Seven months had passed since the collapse of the wall, when in the middle of the night, or so I thought because I was asleep in my cot, there was a great fuss suddenly in progress. Without going into detail which I still vividly remember, my mother was in labour.

My grandmother, who still lived downstairs, was informed of what was happening and she agreed to 'keep an eye' on me. This grandmother was completely different in one respect to my maternal grandmother, who at the slightest inkling that something was amiss, usually concerning the grandchildren, would arrive on the front doorstep to help, whether or not her assistance was required. But 'Little Nanny' was not so forward as she and would wait to be asked. My mother told me that in the early days of her marriage she often found 'Little Nanny' sitting on the bottom stair listening to the latest innovation which my parents had acquired, namely the 'wireless'. But she would not accept their invitation to go upstairs and listen in comfort.

On the night in question she doubtless kept an eye on me, but come morning her concentration must have slipped because I was up, dressed and out before she knew of it. My father arrived home to make sure I was all right, just at the moment it was discovered that I was missing. They knew immediately where I would be found, and when my father raced hotfoot to my other grandmother's, there I was enjoying her hospitality.

In today's climate it seems it is becoming increasingly risky to allow young children out of one's sight for fear of heavy traffic, abduction etc., but not so then. There was hardly any traffic and children went about by themselves, not continually accompanied by their parents. There must have been exceptions but as a general rule children seem to have been much safer.

Anyway, there I was, safe and sound. I was told that I had a baby brother, but I would not be allowed to see him until my father and I went to the hospital to fetch him and my mother home. Obviously the baby could not be brought out for me to see, and child visitors were not allowed in the hospital, so – end of story, as we say. Nowadays one is often told that not being able to see the new baby will affect the bonding between baby and other siblings, with the result that children are often allowed in close proximity to the new infant quite soon after the baby is born. I can only answer that from the day my father and I fetched my mother and baby brother home from the hospital I just absolutely adored him. My mother would tell people from that day on he had two mothers.

Not that adoration would have been the best word to describe my reaction the day I was told I had a new baby brother. I had woken to find myself alone, and although I was probably aware that my parents had gone to get this new baby for me, it must be noted that this was at a time when small children were not enlightened as to where babies came from. I had been spoiled as the only child until then, not only by my parents but by two of my mother's younger sisters, not so much by receiving material gifts but certainly by love and attention. Suddenly that day there was all the fuss and upheaval because a new baby was to be 'got' and I well and truly had my nose put out of joint.

Children, as we all know, are great little actors and I would have been making full use of the 'Nobody loves me now' plaintive call. I announced that I never wanted to go home again. Which confirms how very upset I must have been because home was where I always wanted to be.

However, all was resolved and with a little bribery I was placated, with no adverse effect on my feelings for the new baby. My father and I had lunch with my grandparents, and the bribery mentioned was in effect to give rise to my new routine of having lunch with my grandparents every Sunday for the next six years. It was the Blitz on London in 1940 which eventually caused my visits to cease.

I had two cousins only one and two years younger than myself, and after a few years they would join me on Sunday mornings. We were great friends, particularly the older of the two, who is a girl, and sometimes she would join me for lunch with our grandparents.

I was eleven years old when this routine ceased but during its six years' duration it was a source of great pleasure for me. After Sunday lunch I would trot off to Sunday school while Big Nanny washed up. Then we would sometimes get a bus to the cemetery and I would help her tidy up her elder son's grave and put fresh flowers on it. I hope that doesn't sound too morbid because I remember it being a very pleasant, peaceful time and I enjoyed these

70

trips with my grandmother. We didn't always go to the cemetery, on rare occasions we would go to the cinema. Oh how my grandmother loved the cinema, and we liked each other's company very much.

5

I Want to Go Home

Life for my family followed a completely new routine after the birth of my brother. We were still living upstairs, with the only access to the water supply downstairs, but somehow my mother coped wonderfully. This situation was not unusual at that time. Most houses had a family living downstairs and another occupying the upstairs, unless they were a large family which would occupy the whole house.

It was at that time in the 1930s that suburbia began to grow rapidly. Many families moved out to the new council estates but many moved to the newly built private estates too. In the early days of my marriage we bought a house on one of these private estates in North London. A neighbour told me that when they were first built, many of the houses had been bought by families like her own, which, because of their size, required a whole house and it had become as cheap to buy as to rent.

My father wanted to move out to one of these estates but my mother, not wanting to isolate herself from her close-knit family, did not. I have always been thankful that she won the day, familiar persons and familiar places have always meant a great deal to me.

By this time I was settled in school and was very happy there, often bringing a friend home as we returned from morning school at lunch-time to have a quick peep at my new baby until either Mum put a stop to it or the novelty wore off.

Our house was the first one in the street but it was about a third of the distance up the street. I say 'up' because we always referred to the main road as being the bottom of the street and the other end as the top. The first third of the street was the site of the baker's shop and garden. Then came the ten houses and at the top the local dairy and its premises for milk delivery.

It was decided that I should be allowed to wheel my brother in his pram when time allowed. Not near the bottom of the street because of the traffic, which included single-decker buses, but up the street and along the T-junction at the top because this area saw very little traffic.

As I write this account I still find it difficult to believe that a child of five and a half years of age was allowed unaccompanied to wheel a baby in his pram. But I did just that. I would wheel him up and down the street, and even back and forth along the road at the top under the watchful eye of the small shopkeepers there.

As the purpose of this was usually to lull the baby to sleep, as is the regular reason for such an activity, I was always reluctant to take him home while he was still awake. My mother continually went to the front door and marvelled at my patience pushing him back and forth, but children love to feel they are being helpful and I was proud when neighbours wanted to see him.

My best friend lived next door. She lived upstairs, as we did. She did not attend my school but we spent a great deal of time together outside of school hours. We were very unsophisticated as children and for years played with our dolls and prams. We would accompany our mothers when they went shopping, more often than not pushing our dolls' prams. Small girls were still doing this when my daughters were young and both my daughters pushed their dolls

73

around the shops. But this was before supermarkets came into being, a time when most mothers would shop for fresh food every day.

Suddenly I became the proud owner of a real baby to take for walks, something my friend did not achieve until she was ten years old, just when they were moving a short distance away.

She would often accompany me when I was pushing my 'real' pram. She was allowed to rest her hand on the handle but I would not let her take complete control. However, one day I was not quite ready when she called for me and by the time I emerged from the front door I found that my mother had allowed her to push the pram on her own.

Outside my house was a drain in the gutter and I must have been beside myself with jealousy because I can vividly recall walking to the edge of the pavement, opening my tiny handbag and tipping the meagre contents down the drain. Not satisfied with this, when I obtained possession of the pram and baby, using them as a guided missile I chased my friend up the street. I was obviously not the nicest child around.

What a sensible lady my mother was. First, she allowed me to do all manner of things for the new baby, keeping her eagle eye on me the whole time, and second, I spent a lot of time with her when the baby was tucked up in his cradle for the night.

Babysitters were unheard of in those days, but my father took on this role. Because I was at school I was unable to attend the afternoon get-togethers at Big Nanny's and my mother was probably unable, with the new baby, to spare the time. So, she and I would often go in the early evening to visit my grandparents or an aunt and uncle. By the time my father returned from work, my brother would be in bed, my mother and I had already eaten and my father's meal would be on the table, so off we would go. The outing would not last long, but for an hour or so I was being given a treat and the baby was not the centre of attention.

Occasionally, if there was a suitable film being shown, my mother and I would visit the cinema. I think this must have been during school holidays because when we returned my father would have a snack meal ready for the three of us, which would have meant that I went to bed much later than usual.

A great deal of leisure time was spent visiting relatives or relatives visiting our home. It mattered not where the venue was, we knew what we would be eating for Sunday tea. The only Sunday lunch which would be eaten away from our own home was when Big Nanny and Grandad did the entertaining. As I have already said, I was the exception to this, going there every Sunday for lunch.

To return to Sunday tea. Wherever it took place every person had by his plate a smaller plate or saucer on which was a china egg-cup and a pin. In each egg-cup there was a tiny amount of vinegar. All this preparation was for the winkles, which had to be extracted from their shells. There were also shrimps, brown and pink. Occasionally there were prawns. These delicacies were very fresh, having been bought that morning from the regular Sunday stalls. Thinly sliced white bread, very crusty and covered with seeds, accompanied these, and to follow there was always a lovely home-made cake. It never varied. Does this mean it was a boring way of life or did it contribute to an emotionally contented way of life? I believe the latter, but it is probably a generation difference and the younger persons in our society would I am sure disagree.

Something which we did quite often was to take a day trip to the seaside. Only a few hundred yards from our home was a newsagent's where in later years one could book

75

theatre seats for the West End shows. But when I was a child it was the establishment where we booked seats on a coach for a Sunday trip to the sea. We would board the coach outside the newsagents', and it was all very convenient and exciting. I made more of these trips than the rest of my family because a lady and gentleman living a few houses further up the street had one child, a girl who was about six years older than me. They would often take me with them on their excursions as company for their daughter. I can only suppose that having a playmate on the beach who is six years younger than yourself is, for a child, better than having no playmate.

It was some years later that I realised how well-respected my parents were by the other residents in the street. Particularly my mother by the other ladies. They did not socialise or get together for coffee mornings but would be ready to help when the necessity arose. This was brought home to me when I married. One of the ladies came to our front door one day prior to my wedding and presented me with a beautiful pair of sheets. I was astonished, having rarely spoken to her. She explained it was the least she could do in return for my mother's kindness so often to her when her children were young and she was short of money until her husband was paid his weekly wage. What was so important to this lady was that as well as lending her the necessary small amount of cash, my mother never told anyone else that this kind gesture was necessary.

The next exciting event which was to take place was Auntie Nellie's wedding. I was seven and a half years of age and was to be the chief bridesmaid. There were two bridesmaids and a page-boy – the little trio who regularly kept company on Sunday mornings.

The preparations were many, long and great fun. The flat

where she and her husband would begin their married life was beautifully furnished. I remember it well, in great detail, because it was so different in style to any other homes which I visited. This was 1936, Art Deco had become the fashion and everything was influenced by this, including the dining table centrepiece – a vase of tulips made completely of glass.

We three small cousins were regularly taken to Big Nanny's and from there we accompanied Auntie Nellie to a near neighbour who was the dressmaker. There were a number of these visits, the first one or two taking place in Auntie Nellie's bedroom, but because we used her bed as a trampoline it was decided further fittings would be in the dressmaker's house.

The wedding was on Christmas Day in 1936 and, as were most weddings at that time, the reception was held in the bride's home. Both my grandmother and grandfather were excellent cooks but numbers dictated how much of any roast meal could be fitted in the oven, and quite often the roast potatoes and sometimes the joint of meat also would be taken by Grandad to the baker, who not only opened his shop for business on Sundays, but also allowed the use of his ovens to facilitate the cooking of the Sunday roast for local families. Large pans of potatoes well-greased with beef-dripping and covered with pristine white tea-cloths would be carried to the baker's by Grandad and collected by him when cooked.

Needless to say, this was to be the way the wedding breakfast, which was also Christmas lunch, was to be catered for. Nowadays most people will hire caterers for the event but then the family usually did the work themselves. There appears to have been a compromise at this event, because two neighbours were engaged for the day to pre-pare and serve the meal etc. The baker's ovens must have been well used that day, for about forty persons attended the wedding. The photographs were taken in the garden, with the principal participants seated in the front. It was a lovely day which Auntie Nellie richly deserved.

Everyone had a good time and it went on in the evening until well past my cousin's and my bedtime, so it was decided that we two would be put to bed. Unfortunately, we were allocated a share in the bed of a very large elderly lady who I can only suppose had decided it was way past her bedtime too.

Whether my cousin and I protested at being sent up to bed because we thought it was too early or because we had no wish to share the bed of the lady who was unknown to us or because we did not wish to leave the party, I know not. I do know, however, that we were put to bed and placated by each being given a glass of Grandad's ginger cordial which he always made. How I would love to possess his recipe. Immediately I had an accident, and spilled the whole glass. What a mess. There can be few drinks as sticky as Grandad's ginger cordial.

My aunt and uncle did not go on a honeymoon that day but were going to their newly furnished flat the following day. As usually happens with family parties, the old and the young go home first and the jollification gradually winds down. My parents and my brother had gone home and I awoke to discover this. I immediately began my usual plaintive cry of, 'I want to go home.' Auntie Nellie, the happy bride, had to take me home. Once again she came to my rescue. I was without doubt called a nuisance and a 'wimp' or the 1936 equivalent. My cousin would not remain in the bed without me and she had to be taken home also. Fortunately she lived just round the corner, her garden backing on to my grandparents' garden. I imagine the big elderly lady was pleased to be shot of us. To this day I do not know who she was.

*

Living in London at that time was like living in a village. Everything one required was within walking distance. There was no necessity to travel out of your own London borough unless you were visiting something or someone for a particular reason.

Not only were there never-ending shops in the main road at the bottom of my street, there were two markets, one only five minutes' walk one way and the other five minutes' walk the other way. Both sides of the road housing these markets were also non-stop rows of shops. Not that we thought of these as the shopping centre. That was less than five minutes' walk in another direction. There one found the department store and all the well-known chain stores as well as numerous private shops.

It was all terribly parochial. A good example of this was the dairy, which was actually situated at the top of the street. It was an establishment which only bottled the milk and delivered it daily to the customers. It had no shop attached where one could buy dairy products. If they were required, there was the grocer's only twenty yards away. The dairy delivered my mother's daily bottles of milk for as long as I can remember. But one day, not many moons ago, during one of my regular trips to visit them I was amazed to find that my parents' refrigerator was stocked with the week's milk supply in plastic bottles. I queried this due to the fact that my mother had always insisted her milk be delivered each day, and in bottles to boot. I was informed that the dairy had closed and she had decided to purchase her milk supply weekly at the supermarket. I reminded her that at the top of the street, around the corner, only one hundred yards from her dairy was another. It was a lovely shop which sold all dairy products and also had a daily milk delivery side to the business. My mother just looked at me with an incredulous look on her face and said, 'But that isn't my dairy.' Yes, parochial is the correct description.

One also experienced a wonderful feeling of continuity.

The church I attended regularly at three o'clock every Sunday was the church where my parents were married. I have the seventy-seven-year-old church magazine announcing the marriage. My brother and I and our cousins were baptised there. I was also a Brownie at this church.

In the Guiding Movement one becomes a Girl Guide at the age of eleven, before that a Brownie and now, even younger than the Brownies, are the Rainbows. But when I was a child the first organised group were the Brownies. Then as now the leader of the group was called Brown Owl. The pack must have been quite large because we also had a Tawny Owl and a Speckley Owl to help run it. I have their autographs in my autograph book. Brown Owl wrote: 'Judge not those you meet by their appearance. Find out their virtues for yourself.'

One gets the impression now that young children spend a considerable amount of time watching television or sitting in front of a computer. When we were children there was a children's programme on the radio, but apart from this there could have been very little else which would have been of great enough interest to the very young for them to sit all evening just listening intently.

Perhaps this is why we joined a variety of activities. After school every Friday my friend who lived next door and I would return to my school to attend a hive of activity called Play-centre. I cannot recollect doing anything more exciting than singing, painting and playing board games. But we obviously enjoyed it. From there we went to Brownies, I was a Fairy and she was a Pixie.

As Brownies we were not an isolated group but part of the whole church organisation. Once again it seems that more fun can be had when there is a mix of age and ability taking part than when individual age groups segregate themselves.

A superb example of this was a production of *Snow-White and the Seven Dwarfs* which was put on by the church. It was I believe mainly the Scouts, Girl Guides and other young adult members of the church who were participating in the show. It was quite a large production involving many people, with the Brownies acting the parts of the birds and rabbits, who in the story help Snow-White spring-clean the Dwarfs' house. The bigger Brownies were the rabbits and the smaller were the birds. This included me – I was a bird. The birds wore brown cotton leotards and brown cotton caps with huge bright yellow peaks representing the beaks.

We practised and we practised our part in the pantomime. We sang and we danced to the song 'The Dicky Bird Hop' by Ronald Gorley. I had always remembered the words to the song but never realised it was so well known a piece of music until some years ago when I heard on the radio that the writer of the song had died.

When we attended rehearsals we Brownies always waited for the part in the pantomime when a very tall young man who was acting the part of one of the Dwarfs rode around the stage on a child's tiny tricycle. With his knees touching his chin he would ring the tricycle bell loudly.

There was, however, one very embarrassing moment for my parents. When the birds and rabbits danced out on to the stage, I was the only one who had forgotten to remove her socks and shoes. I imagine it caused quite a lot of laughter from the audience – a bird in socks and shoes.

About this time the family had another surprise. One of my mother's sisters produced twins. Only one baby was expected, so this was a cause for great excitement. Two little girls arrived unexpectedly and they were beautiful.

I had been initiated into the baby 'business' with the arrival of my brother three or four years earlier and had enjoyed it, so needless to say I was soon to be found, time permitting, helping my aunt with the twins.

I accompanied her to the local baby clinic and would assist in the undressing of the infants and taking them to be weighed. I was quite used to handling the babies, and my aunt was obviously confident that I could be trusted with them. I remember one day at the clinic when I was undressing one of the babies, a nurse or more probably a health visitor came over and questioned whether I was old enough to be doing this. My aunt replied that I was very capable and that I always helped with the babies. She, my mother and the other siblings took after my grandmother in being very forthright.

There has been a whooping-cough vaccination available for many years now, but this was not always so and when persons occasionally question the necessity for this vaccination, they should be reminded that sometimes whooping cough was fatal, as it was in the case of one of my lovely twin cousins at the age of ten months. The hospital was only one hundred yards away and my auntie would visit to breast-feed the baby but unfortunately the child died.

Another much dreaded disease in past years was diphtheria. I recall my mother taking my brother and me to the local clinic, where we were given the diphtheria immunisation. After the terrifying jab I was given a sweet by a mechanical nodding duck.

The subject of contagious diseases brings to mind the instance when I contracted chicken pox. Being five and a half years older than my brother, I was at school and might have been expected to catch children's diseases and to infect my brother with them, which happened in the case of chicken pox. I only had a few spots and at the time the fact that, due to infection, I had to retain a story book which belonged to the school was far more important to me than the disease. But I passed on the horrible itchy malady to my brother, who was less than one year old, and because he was so covered with the rash of spots the doctor advised my mother to pour the soothing lotion on a large piece of cloth and roll the baby gently over it.

My brother contracted mumps but this time not from me. I never had the disease as a child, consequently when my own children caught it they passed it on to me.

The occasion when my brother was infected I vividly recall because my grandmother, who was living downstairs, came up to see my brother. This was unusual in itself because she never ventured upstairs and for certain never interfered in any way. But she came up this day to look after us while my mother popped around the corner to the doctor's surgery to request a home visit. I remember Little Nanny telling my mother that it was a pity Dr Jelly wasn't still available because he was a wonderful doctor and very good with children.

Now for a young child to hear of a Dr Jelly, it must have conjured up all kinds of pictures in my mind. I recall repeatedly asking who was this Dr Jelly, but I was only informed that he was an old doctor from way back. My mother and Little Nanny were concentrating on my sick brother at the time.

But as soon as possible I went downstairs to ask my grandmother for more information on this Dr Jelly. She was not very forthcoming but said my father would be able to tell me more. So next I approached Dad, and he told me a number of humorous stories concerning the doctor. Since then research has revealed a great deal more information about the good doctor for whom my grandmother had such a high regard.

Little Nanny, it seems, swore by Dr Jelly, who was born in 1866. He took pharmaceutical examinations at eighteen years of age and examinations in medicine, surgery and midwifery at forty-five.

At this time in a rich district a doctor would charge a guinea or more a visit. This would enable him to live in a comfortable manner, whereas in a poorer neighbourhood the work would be more arduous and the reward smaller. So wealthy practices were sought after, while the poor were left to doctors who were young, inexperienced, perhaps lacked financial backing or, as seems to be Dr Jelly's reason, wished to be of service where he was most needed.

Dr Jelly had qualified in 1910, before Lloyd George brought in national health insurance. Then and even after, provision of medical attention for the poorer members of society was not good. A half-a-crown charge for the doctor's home visit was a lot to a family whose weekly income might only be a pound. There were friendly societies to which some families would pay twopence or more a week, and this would entitle them to treatment by the society's doctor or the payment of a doctor's fee.

Poverty was the cause of much of the ill health. It was a vicious circle, poverty being the reason for such poor living conditions and inadequate diet and these being the cause of ill health, which contributed to the poverty in these communities. Dr Jelly appears to have recognised this when he prescribed his patients steak instead of recognised pick-me-ups.

He became known as The Threepenny Doctor because he only charged threepence for a home or surgery visit.

There is no doubt that he was an eccentric in the extreme who set about his work with enormous vigour. He quickly saw that two basic problems were diet and the health of women. The latter he solved by offering women help with contraception and childbirth. He was, however, imprisoned for three years in 1916 for the murder of a lady by 'illegal operation'.

But the local people trusted him because of his no-nonsense approach. If a patient was alone and had been told to remain in bed, the doctor would call, let himself in, pick up the empty medicine bottle on the stairs and his threepenny fee, re-fill the bottle and replace it.

My father remembered being about seven years old when he first saw Dr Jelly, who had come on a large bay horse to visit my grandmother. The doctor gave Dad's eldest brother a penny for holding the horse while he was visiting his patient. The next thing my father remembered was seeing him riding around the area on a tricycle.

Controversial is a word which is barely adequate when describing the doctor. He would provoke arguments with discontented patients, members of the public and anyone in authority, and was involved in many court cases in his conflicts with the law. After his period in prison he opened a shop which met the requirements of a surgery in one half of the establishment and sold grocery products in the other. One could also order a suit of clothes. It seems he had learned tailoring during his term of imprisonment. My father said that he employed several machinists and he had had a suit made to measure by him.

Anyone entering his premises in a bowler hat and carrying a walking stick was immediately shown the door, and not in a polite fashion. They would be told, 'Clear off'. He would put up notices warning any persons in authority, inspectors or policemen to keep out.

He would make up his own prescriptions and remedies – as I mentioned before, he had taken his pharmaceutical examinations before becoming a doctor. Patients also valued his opinions, which were often controversial but based on common-sense. His answer to sickly children seems to have been always the same – fresh air, exercise and some good red meat.

It was said that when a doctor visited a patient at home the routine never varied. After being shown into the 'parlour', the doctor would take off his gloves and place them and his walking cane on the table, topped by his top-hat. Then he would ascend to the bedroom to visit the patient, descending later to talk to the wife or whoever, slowly put on his gloves, pick up his walking cane and his hat, say 'Good morning' and leave, still holding the ever-present Gladstone bag.

But not Dr Jelly, he would arrive transported by whichever strange mode of transport was popular with him at the time. He would dash into the house wearing, as always, black clothes and hat, not at all fussy about his appearance and not carrying the usual Gladstone bag. He would carry all kinds of requisites in his pockets. It was not unusual to see him striding along, this very tall figure, with his stethoscope dangling from one of his pockets.

During my research I was interested to learn of a gentleman's experience when, as a young lad serving in a hardware shop, he encountered the doctor, who wanted to purchase twopennyworth of nails. The boy weighed them out and, while he was searching for something in which to wrap them, the doctor scooped them up from the scales and filled his jacket pocket with them.

This story reminded me of my father's experience with nails. As I have already written, after my father and his brothers and sisters were left fatherless they had to learn quickly to become resourceful to assist their mother, who had become the wage-earner in the family. My father became the shoe-repairer and so would often purchase nails.

One day he returned home for lunch and, fancying a piece of steak, he gave one shilling and sixpence to his youngest brother, requesting him to purchase it for him. Unfortunately the boy must have been day-dreaming, as small boys often are, and instead of going to the butcher's for steak he went to the ironmongers' and asked for one and sixpence worth of nails. He was often sent by my father to purchase nails for shoe-repairing. Now, Dr Jelly had

My grandparents. Little Nanny holding the uncle who suffered shell-shock.

Uncle who suffered shell-shock, on the left.

Back row, third from the right, clutching 'the box'.

Uncle in the Salvation Army Band. Centre row, second from right.

The fairy doll in infant school.

With my friend who is wearing the much coveted shoes.

Dad with Billy the goat.

Taking no chances in the deep end.

Auntie Nellie's wedding.

St. Barnabas. The family's church.

The Congregational Church, known as the Round Chapel.

Our 'girls' club. The author far left of front row with her two friends, one standing behind and the other sitting next to her.

obtained a pocketful of two-inch nails for twopence. It doesn't take much imagination to picture how many small and very small nails my uncle was given for one shilling and sixpence.

But to return to Dr Jelly – Dad once visited him because his arm had become infected and was very swollen. The doctor bandaged it, gave him some lint and ointment and it was cured in two or three days. But the reason Dad remembered the event so clearly was because while the doctor was attending to his arm he was also looking after his Christmas puddings, which were happily bubbling away on a coal stove in the corner of the surgery.

But as a doctor, although often in trouble, he won the hearts of the local people and helped his patients in very practical ways. He had been known to comment on the coldness of the patient's bedroom, ask for a bucket, go out and from somewhere fill the bucket with coal, return, kneel down, rake out the ashes and relight the fire. If the family were very poor they were often told to buy the children something to eat with the threepence which should have been his fee.

He clearly was very eccentric and, following his prison sentence, as well as being a tailor, doctor (unregistered) and retailer, he became a coach-tour operator. He bought one or two motor coaches and ran day trips to Southend, but breakdowns were more often than not the order of the day and the whole venture seems to have been rather unsuccessful.

During the Second World War, by which time he was in his seventies, he was still pedalling his way around on a tricycle. It is believed he died in 1946.

I settled down well in the junior school, encouraged by my parents and helped I am certain by the stability of my whole

87

existence. I never moved house until I married. My friends remained constant as did my extended family. My father never changed his job, remaining with the same firm until he retired at sixty years of age. Although not over-friendly – one was not at that time – I was familiar with Dad's bosses and many happy occasions involving the bosses and employees continued to take place regularly. My parents went on the firm's outings when they were courting and often recalled a bad accident in a fun-fair at the seaside during one of the summer coach trips. Fortunately, it did not involve any of their friends.

One of the happy events which I remember well took place in 1937. The venue was the newly built town hall, which was officially opened in July 1937. Whether the assembly rooms were allowed to be used before the official opening or whether the event I remember took place after the opening, I know not. But it must have been soon after Christmas Day 1936, which was the wedding day of Auntie Nellie, because I wore my bridesmaid's dress.

The occasion was a dance and it can be imagined how important I felt in my long pink dress. As my father was quite an important member of the staff, my mother was presented with the largest box of chocolates I have ever seen.

I don't remember going again to the assembly rooms until I was sixteen years of age, when I began going dancing there on most Saturday evenings.

6

Everyone Wanted to Go Home

Life continued in a well-ordered routine.

By then only my grandmother and her youngest daughter were occupying the downstairs of the house. The daughter was soon to be married and then only Little Nanny would be left there.

My father was still resolutely saving for the deposit on a house. He needed fifty pounds and it took him exactly ten years to save this princely sum. He set about looking for a suitable house, although probably not as enthusiastically as one might expect. After all, his place of work was across the road, his club within walking distance and all family and friends were living locally.

My grandmother was beginning to get rather worried about our moving, realising it would mean having new tenants living upstairs.

Whether my father approached the baker who owned the house or whether the baker approached my father, I do not know, but it was decided that my father would buy the house.

Life carried on as usual for a year, by which time my young aunt had married, leaving just my grandmother living downstairs. My parents were becoming anxious for our little family to have the use of the whole house. It is often said that as one door closes another opens and, lo and behold, not only did Little Nanny agree to move, which must have been rather sad for her after living there for nearly forty years, but she married an elderly widower, whom we had all known for many years, and they set up home in another house.

When she moved to her new abode the extended family continued par excellence. Little Nanny and her new husband rented one house, and next door the newly married daughter and her husband occupied the downstairs accommodation and the widowed eldest daughter lived upstairs. When two children were born to the younger daughter, it is not difficult to see why in later years they and their children were always so close to their aunt.

Early on in this story I recalled occasionally taking my mother back to London to visit my elderly aunt and mentioned that her great-niece and great-nephew when they were in their teens visited her during their school lunch break. I venture to suggest that this is what 'family' is all about: youngsters of seventeen years visiting relatives who are in their late eighties, abandoning their school friends for a short while to make certain the elderly great-aunt has an adequate meal.

I enjoyed school routine, of which there was a great deal at the time. Rules, if they are sensible, make for a well-ordered environment in which to work.

Every Friday we were assembled in the hall with our hands held up, palms facing to the front. If the headmistress as she inspected them could see our nails higher than our fingers, they must be cut by Monday morning. It may sound trivial and a rather foolish exercise, but couple that to the other practice – giving a fancy tin box containing a very well-known brand of shoe polish, brushes and polishing cloth every Friday to a girl whose shoes had been nice and clean and shiny all week – and you are encouraging the children to take an interest in their appearance.

I must admit the second of these procedures always puzzled me. To my tiny mind, it seemed to make more sense to give the shoe-polishing items to a girl with grubby shoes who I thought was in need of them. But the school staff probably monitored it well, so that the little gifts were allocated in a fair way. I know at home the family shoe-cleaning equipment was kept in this tin for many years.

As I have already written, I loved school. My mother would complain that I always had my head in a book. My father had obtained three huge encyclopaedias – unfortunately, we did not have a whole set – and I would study them for hours. There were three items of particular interest to me in these books, which were wonderfully illustrated. They were World War I, The Life and Death of Edith Cavell and Greek Mythology. The last I was able to study later in greater detail at school.

When my father died I asked my mother if I might have the books, but Dad had given them to a very good friend of the family.

I spent a lot of time in the local library. Mum would constantly enquire what I did there. In more recent years she would tell me that as a child I was always 'looking up this or that', so I suppose that was my stock answer to her enquiries. But as long as I returned with a book for her written by Ethel M. Dell or Ruby M. Ayres she was satisfied. I have often wondered how often I must have taken home a book which she had already read.

As an ex primary school teacher, I know that a child who does not find the work difficult and therefore may have time to spare can be disruptive in a classroom, and it is the teacher's responsibility to make sure that the child is kept occupied to his or her advantage. My teacher solved this quite often by sitting me at the back of the class with a child who was having a little difficulty, and I could work with her and help her.

I also enjoyed what I considered, or would have done if I had known the description at that time, extra-curricular activities.

One of these was keeping silkworms. A few of us offered to care for two or three silkworms each. We had to house them in a shoe box and feed them on cabbage leaves, but we had been told that their food of choice is actually mulberry leaves.

Now, apart from my friend who lived in the house next to mine, my best friend was the boy whose father was the baker in the corner shop. The end of their garden was separated from our property by a high fence in which a small door had been cut out and hinged to enable easy access to and fro for the baker's son, the boy who lived on the doctor's premises, whose garden also met our garden, and me. We spent a great deal of time together 'swimming' in the pool, which was actually a large bath. In a photograph which I have, I have around my middle a rubber ring which resembles a life-belt. I obviously was not taking any chances!

As well as playing with water we also spent a great deal of our time up a tree which was in the centre of the baker's garden. It had a crazy paving path encircling it and was quite a feature of the garden.

The boy from the doctor's premises was not allowed to climb the tree, for safety reasons, I believe, and I was not supposed to climb it for the very simple reason that it was a mulberry tree and if it was bearing fruit my clothes suffered badly from mulberry juice stains. But it meant I had access to mulberry leaves to the delight of my silkworms.

When the silkworms spun up their cocoons we returned them to school. I am not sure how many of the other children were successful with their silkworms, because I now know that at the stage of transformation when they spin up their cocoons, they are more successful when fed on mulberry leaves.

But some must have survived well on cabbage leaves as it was noted that they were all in white cocoons; mine were in yellow cocoons, and it was decided that feeding on mulberry leaves was the reason. This, however, is not the case. I have been reliably informed that the colour varies naturally, some being white and others yellow, probably due to some genetic variation. So, after all these years, another little question has been answered.

Another example of our interest in natural history was keeping tadpoles in the classroom one year. This comes to mind simply because the tadpoles were just turning into frogs when the time for a school break was at hand. It was probably half-term and not a long break, because a volunteer was needed to care for the tadpoles during the holiday. I, who would always volunteer before I was aware of what I was volunteering for, was allowed to take them home.

Now, tadpoles gradually become frogs when they are still not much more than a centimetre long, and they hop. I decided one of the minute frogs was missing and was sure it had hopped out somewhere between the front door and our flat upstairs. Consternation and tears from me, and practically hysterics from my grandmother at the thought of a frog being somewhere in her flat downstairs until she was informed of its actual size.

When I was teaching, never a year passed when we did not have caterpillars which emerged as butterflies the following spring and frog spawn which eventually produced the tiny frogs. But I had learned my lesson as a child and, as soon as the four legs appeared, the frogs were given a rock higher than the water, on which they sat quite happily, and the fish tank was covered by a piece of net. If one did inadvertently escape, all the children would sit quite still until I found it. I can't remember that we were ever unsuccessful. Then I would take the tiny frogs home and put them in my pond.

We did have one happening which, although a success, had a rather unfortunate ending. So that we might be lucky enough to see the butterflies actually emerge, I had the jam jar housing the cabbage white caterpillar chrysalises on my desk, visible to all eager little eyes. We were in luck that day and both butterflies came out and prepared themselves for flight.

This school was deep in the heart of the countryside and one end of my classroom had huge windows which opened out on to the farmer's field. We all gathered in front of the windows. I opened one wide and took off the lid of the jam jar, whereupon both butterflies flew out, two birds swooped down and that was the end of the butterflies. A very subdued class went back to their seats.

Every child has a natural gift of some kind. They may be academic, arty, good at sport or their talents may lean towards other interests or abilities, and it is the teacher's responsibility to seek these out, note them and encourage them. But it is also the parents' responsibility, and to do the job properly time is of the essence, and time is the commodity which is nowadays in such short supply. Time, that is, to sit down with the children or accompany them during their activities and not just deposit them.

Many parents spend a considerable amount of their time and money taking the children to organised activities. But so many children take for granted that their free time will be filled with pursuits and entertainment, that to return home after school and occupy themselves with or without assistance from a parent is quite often not at all to their liking.

Both parents often go out to work now, some of necessity,

94

others because they wish to. The children who always find a parent, usually the mother, at home to welcome them are becoming fewer. When I was a child the majority of mothers did not go out to work. Many mothers would do work at home which would require little expertise and would fit in nicely with their domestic arrangements, at the same time supplementing the family income.

I consider myself extremely lucky in having had a wonderful nuclear and extended family life in which I was encouraged and given the confidence which is of such benefit to a child. This was backed up by the attitude of the school.

I was a very young member of my class and also quite small for my age when it was decided that I could go swimming. But unlike the open-air pools where one could gradually immerse oneself in the water by walking down a slope into the pool, this was an indoor pool which was three feet deep at the shallow end. It was agreed that I should wear a rubber ring for safety. The lady who was the instructor would drop me in and someone, perhaps the teacher, would be in the water ready to 'save' me I suppose. I can remember thinking it was good fun. Once again, my mother was a little concerned but my father was all for it.

Another incident of encouragement which remains with me vividly, so vividly in fact that to this day I cringe when I think of it, concerns the piano.

My parents had bought a piano with the idea in mind that I should learn to play it at a young age. Unfortunately, I had not got around to having lessons, but I would play with one finger 'by ear' and would thump away with my left hand. My father would show me the notes for certain tunes and one of my favourites was 'Men of Harlech'.

One day the teacher, who was the regular piano player at assembly, asked if there was a pupil who would be willing to play on the piano a tune to which the assembled pupils could leave the hall. I immediately thought of 'Men of Harlech' and volunteered my services. The teacher probably had the idea that I was having piano lessons and duly sat me at the piano, and I played the tune with my right hand and thumped away with my left.

It must have been an awful noise but the teacher pretended to appreciate it by asking me to play at the following morning's assembly. What an understanding lady she must have been to encourage a child who was giving such a dismal performance but who was obviously keen.

I actually did not go to piano lessons until I was twelve years of age but in the meantime I took to playing by tonic sol-fa. I would buy second-hand pieces of sheet music from the local bookshop and would occasionally obtain a book of songs which was given away free with a comic or a magazine. I still possess two of these, one containing Arthur Askey's songs and another containing songs by George Formby. Both have tonic sol-fa as well as piano music.

Sometimes in the middle of a song it would go completely wrong. It took me some time to work out that I always played in what I later learned was the key of C, and when the tune went wrong it was because the music had changed to a different key.

I was also fond of poetry or so I am told. Whether for writing a piece or for reciting I know not, but I was presented with a book by someone from the LCC. The book was the *Ingoldsby Legends* and it has always been a mystery to me why they should give such a tome to a nine year old. To this day I have never read it, as it is enough to inhibit any enthusiasm for poetry I might have had. I am certain the intention to encourage was good – it was just a little optimistic on the part of someone.

There are only two poems which mean a great deal to me and which I remember word for word.

One is 'Jim' by Hilaire Belloc, about a boy 'who ran away from his nurse, and was eaten by a lion' and ends with the well-known lines: 'And always keep a-hold of Nurse / For fear of finding something worse.'

Mum often recited it to me from when I was a very small child and this rendering always took place while she was washing me. Over and over again I heard it. I was enthralled by it. Eventually I knew it off by heart, but was not aware for many years that it was a very well-known poem by a very well-known poet.

My experiences relating to poetry were not always so pleasant. One day I climbed the stairs to the roof of the school to visit the toilets, which were situated there. I must have been up there some considerable time because the teacher came up to find me. This wasn't too difficult because I was reciting 'I Wandered Lonely as a Cloud' when I was 'yanked' out unceremoniously.

This teacher was quite strict and her method of punishment was for the pupil to put her hands on her head, then they would be smacked with the teacher's wooden ruler. Quite lightly, I am sure, because it was accepted without a great deal of fuss.

A bell was always rung in the hall to announce the end of each lesson. The doors to the classrooms being along one side of the hall, everyone could hear it. Where we were or what my class was engaged in I do not know, but one day when the bell sounded I thought it was the end of the school day and I was halfway across the playground when the teacher grabbed me, marched me upstairs, ignored my protestations and gave me the usual hands on head and ruler treatment.

It was a genuine mistake on my part, and my mother made it her business to meet the teacher at the school gate and have a quiet word with her.

I continued to spend a great deal of time with my father, although too old by then to be taken by him to see the ducks on Clapton pond. He would often recall the times he spent with me visiting those ducks. It seems they were a great favourite with me when I was very small, causing great excitement if they were walking on the frozen pond instead of swimming. He must have spent many very uncomfortable hours looking at those ducks in the winter, because he hated the cold weather and feeling cold. It is a fact that I cannot recall ever hearing him complain about the heat.

He was a very gentle man and although he had known poverty when a child, he never thought that this was so. He was of the opinion that his childhood had been very happy, and at the end of the day isn't this the most important factor? He quietly went about his business of working during the day and running his small printing enterprise in his spare time until he succeeded in putting down the deposit for his own house. I cannot recall the printing continuing for long after that. The war began two years later and I believe his printing press was sold by then. But he continued with his carpentry up in Big Nanny's loft.

I find it difficult to find suitable words to explain the varying attitudes which are expounded by people comparing life before the Second World War and now.

When they talk about the 'bad old days' I think they are usually referring to inadequate social services, inadequate family income etc., which come under the heading of material things. But when others talk of the 'good old days' they are usually referring to moral issues – the principles of right or wrong behaviour.

Materially, things have improved and we all have a much better 'standard of living'. But this has been gradually coming about since the First World War and many, many people in similar circumstances to my father set about improving their own lot in life. What is more, like my father they did it without sacrificing their 'quality of life', which is the fundamental issue when people talk of the 'good old days'.

Respect for others is on the decline, which is hardly surprising when so many people appear to have so little respect even for themselves. Bad language is the norm, particularly in the younger generation. Abuse of their bodies with drugs and alcohol is increasing.

When I said that my father was gentle, I should have added 'and nice'. What an inadequate word 'nice' is, but I cannot think of an alternative. He did not drink, and if he had any aggression he disposed of it in the boxing ring. As for swearing – no, he did not. He used two words which always amused me. If he considered one was being unreasonable, he would tell that person not to be 'potty', and if he thought something was really lovely or tasty he would refer to it as 'scrumptious'. Yes, he was a 'nice' man.

One often hears older people talking of their childhood and referring to the chores which they had to undertake regularly as children. Maybe this was and is still necessary in a large family. I was fortunate in that I was never asked to do any housework whatsoever. On the other hand, we were not allowed to make unnecessary work for my mother. I remember once, when a teenager, forgetting to put away my shoes. My mother happened to go into my bedroom and as I went down the stairs the shoes swiftly followed me.

Nothing will ever shake me in my belief that a little spoiling of one's children even when they are adult is right. Not by spending a lot of money buying them material things but by giving them lots of love and understanding and yes, by waiting on them in little ways to make sure they are happy. In return parents have the right to respect from their children.

Until I married, my mother gave me breakfast in bed every Sunday. We probably both benefited from this procedure. I was able to have a lie-in and she was able to carry on with her chores without me arriving late for breakfast – she was a great stickler for routine.

There were two little jobs which I did every week when very young. I paid the paper bill, and I took the old battery from the radio to be re-charged and collected the re-charged battery from the previous week. I only recently discovered that the latter was a task given to many of my contemporaries.

Living in an extended family gave children a very stable background – a very orderly existence. Father went to work, and mother kept house and had her relatives for company. Excursions were for parents and children. I can never remember my parents going out alone – we were never left in any other person's charge. But I would often accompany one parent while the other stayed at home.

A great treat for me was to accompany my father to the cinema. I only did this a few times – it had to be a very special film which tempted Dad to the cinema, and when I was nine years of age two films come to mind that did just that.

At that time, as I have said, the main meal was eaten at lunch-time, and on these two occasions I remember being very concerned that my father would not be able to have his tea. Probably to satisfy me, my father was given sandwiches after lunch, to take with him to stave off the pangs of hunger as he was going to the cinema straight from work.

I had my tea on these occasions and then crossed the main road to stand patiently waiting for him to emerge from his place of work. We then set off for the cinema, the first time to see *Gunga Din* and the second time to see *The*

Four Feathers. Both were fabulous films which I have seen again quite recently on television.

It was about this time, not long before the start of the Second World War, that my friend who lived next door and I were initiated into the weekly routine of visiting the public baths alone, not accompanied by our mothers as had been the norm until then. Occasionally we went to the large baths which housed a large section containing the washing baths as well as two swimming pools which we regularly visited. But usually we went a few hundred yards to smaller facilities.

For anyone who has never paid a visit to these establishments I must clear up any misapprehensions which may exist. They were well run, beautifully clean and hygienic and, most important, they were warm. We knew many people who were regular visitors to these facilities although they had bathrooms in their own homes, for the simple reason that very few people had central heating and their bathrooms were cold.

As well as the private bathroom facility, one was given a small portion of soap and a towel. We did not use either, we used our own washing requisites. The soap we took home during the war to be grated up and used in the weekly wash when soap was in short supply. The towel we draped over the wooden draining board on which we stood when getting out of the bath.

If one required more hot or cold water one would call out and ask the attendant for it. She would turn it on from outside the cubicle and it would come gushing out of four-inch-wide taps.

When my friend and I went for our weekly bath on Saturday mornings, the lady was very patient, but if we called out twice she would inform us that we were not getting any more water and we would be told to hurry up.

I realised when I married and for the first time lived in a house which possessed a bathroom, how fortunate I had been until that time in my washing and bathing routine. Until then, when I descended each morning to wash and have breakfast, the kitchen was warm and welcoming. It was also a living room complete with fireside chairs and in the winter the fire would already be lit. That is what a kitchen should be. And once a week a visit to the public baths completed our personal hygiene.

The first bathroom I encountered had hot water supplied by a gas heater which heated the water to the bathroom basin, the bath and the kitchen sink. Unfortunately, it was only lit once a week for our weekly bath and therefore there was no hot water in the bathroom basin or in the kitchen. Not that anyone would have wanted to wash in the freezing cold bathroom. For that matter, it was no fun washing in the cold miserable little kitchenette which was really a scullery and which, apart from the old gas cooker, was equipped with exactly the same items that were housed in my mother's wash-house. No, definitely my first experience of a bathroom was not a happy one. I missed the gushing hot water and the central heating of the public baths.

One of our regular Saturday visits to the baths is recalled vividly to mind by a very sad event.

A new Royal Navy submarine called *HMS Thetis* was scheduled for diving trials in June 1939. By then it was becoming clear to most people that there was soon going to be a war with Germany, and when *Thetis* went to sea she was carrying an extra fifty men, including Admiralty experts and also future submarine commanding officers who were there to gain observational experience for when their boats were ready.

102

They arrived at their diving position but things went wrong and *Thetis* went down bow first and hit the bottom at 160 feet with her bow embedded in the mud.

The news of this dreadful disaster was on the radio and I heard it. The drama was heightened when an aunt came to my home and told us of a local young woman whose husband was one of the submariners on board the *Thetis*.

The BBC announced that HMS Submarine *Thetis* had failed to surface. At low tide the stern was eighteen feet above water and the rescuers outside must have felt so helpless, knowing that the trapped men inside were so near yet so far from rescue.

I remember learning that there was only a certain amount of air inside the submarine and unless a rescue was successful before the crew's air was exhausted the men would perish.

Rescuers hammered on the hull but were not certain whether or not they heard a faint tapping in reply. However, they were sure it was not regular Morse Code.

My friend and I trotted off to the baths, doubtless rushing through out ablutions that day, seeing that we were keen to get home and hear how the rescue was progressing.

When we arrived home no successful rescue had been announced and my father was of the opinion that the air had run out.

The large crowd gathered outside the shipyard were told by Cammell Laird's company secretary, 'I am sorry, but there is no hope for the men remaining in the submarine. The best you can do is disperse quietly.'

In the afternoon a statement was issued from Whitehall 'The Admiralty regrets that hope of saving lives in the *Thetis* must be abandoned.'

Only four men had managed to escape – ninety-nine perished.

It may seem strange that a nine-year-old girl should

remember it so clearly but I believe my father is the reason for this; he made sure we were fully aware of such events and this became even more evident after the commencement of World War II.

The evacuation of school children got under way when war was imminent. It was decided that I should be evacuated with school friends, and preparations were made, I imagine not without a great deal of optimism on the part of my parents. I was hardly renowned for staying away from home. But before we set off on Friday September 1st 1939 it was decided that as my brother was not yet of school age, my mother and I could join the group of mothers and children who were going on the Sunday instead.

This we did and we were actually on the train going to East Anglia when war was declared, but it was only when we alighted that we were informed of the fact. We were all transported to a small village called Outwell, a few miles from Wisbech on the Norfolk border, and assembled in the very new school. Then we were gradually sent off to stay with families who had kindly offered to take us in.

We three were very fortunate in that an elderly couple who did not really want any evacuees agreed to take us when the authorities were running short of accommodation. We were very lucky to be sent there, they were a lovely couple. Their daughter and her family lived in the village, and the daughter had a daughter a little older than me. During the very short time we were there we played together.

There were not very many of us – it was, after all, a very small village at that time to accommodate hordes of evacuees – and I don't think it was ever going to be a great success with the mothers who had so much time on their hands. The thing which I remember caused us so much amusement was the village shop. For some unknown reason the mothers thought it was hilarious. It seemed to sell everything although it was very small. Outside, it had ladies' fancy aprons (worn by all housewives) and saucepans hanging side by side.

It was a beautiful village. The house in which we were billeted was in a road going out of the village. The dwellings were few and far between and surrounded by farms. We had great fun watching and 'helping' the farm-workers building haystacks. I never told anyone, but I did come close to having a nasty accident on one of these haystacks. It was in the process of being built and a few of us were sitting on the top when I decided to jump down to the next level, only to find I had landed next to a scythe which was lying there. 'A miss is as good as a mile' we often say, and children do come perilously close to danger so often.

Looking out from the front of the house, we could see the houses on the other side, but separating the two sides of the road was the river, down which ducks and swans would make their way. It was all very picturesque but not what we were used to, particularly in the dusk when bats would fly around while we were out for an evening stroll.

We had arrived on the Sunday and on the following Saturday, as a small group of us were strolling along beside the river in the direction of the village, we suddenly recognised my father in the distance, walking towards us. He had journeyed up by train.

I am certain that, although small, 'our' village had a railway station, because my mother often spoke of the kindness of a member of the railway station staff. It seems one young mother in our group had two or three very young children and after a few days was desperate to return home to London. Unfortunately, she did not possess the fare, but when she went to make enquiries regarding trains and fares, a very kind member of staff, understanding her predicament, told her that if she and the little ones got to the station at a certain terribly early hour he would see that they were put on the milk train to London. This they did.

To return to my father's visit. My mother always said she was quite sure the other ladies in the group were as pleased to see him as she was, and our very kind hosts gave him accommodation for the night.

Everyone badgered him with questions. You could have been forgiven for thinking that they had been away from London not for a week but for years. I cannot think what my father's ideas must have been when he thought of Norfolk but he arrived with the whole past week's supply of his daily newspaper to keep us in touch with what had been happening since we had left home. It was when my mother realised that he seemed to have had nothing to eat but eggs and bacon since then, that she decided enough was enough and we would return home. Truth to tell, everyone wanted to go home.

This we did on the Tuesday, but we remained in touch with our hosts for many years. Well, to be accurate, my parents did. As a family we all journeyed up by coach a few times during the following few years but my parents continued the friendship driving up there after the war had ended and my father was the owner of a car. The elderly couple who had been such lovely hosts to us died, but my parents continued to visit their daughter and her family. It was a friendship which lasted for over thirty years.

When we returned home, things had changed even in that short time of ten days. My father had acquired an allotment and there was to be no commencement of the new school year – the children and teachers had mostly been evacuated, although I do not recall a great number who stayed away for any length of time.

One day an elderly gentleman approached us in the street

and asked a few of us where we lived and went to talk to our parents. It seemed he was a teacher close to retirement age who did not wish to be evacuated with his school. The authorities had given him permission to use the school cookery department – a small building adjacent to the school – to teach any children willing to attend. My friends and I were very soon enrolled and Mr Sparrow, for that was his name, did a very useful service in keeping us occupied.

Then the Anderson shelter arrived. There can be few people who were around at the beginning of the Second World War who do not know what an Anderson shelter is. For younger readers, John Anderson Waverley was Home Secretary from 1930–40, and the air-raid shelter issued during his term in office was known as the Anderson shelter.

One had to have a garden to accommodate it. We had a garden but not a large one, and my father, like so many other householders, was not too happy. However, he appreciated the necessity for the shelter, which was large enough to accommodate bunks down either side. Steps led down into it, the floor being about three feet below ground level. The base and right around the four sides was lined, if my memory serves me correctly, with about six inches of concrete. The structure itself was made of corrugated iron.

But before our garden was dug up to erect the shelter, a conversation took place between my father and the baker. As I have already said, the end of the baker's garden met the side of our property – separated by a high fence. It seems the baker was not to be allocated an Anderson shelter because his premises included a cellar which in itself would be shelter of a kind.

It was decided that our shelter be put in the baker's garden and he and his family would be able to use it if the necessity arose. Of course, I do not think anyone then thought that the time would come during the war when we

107

would be obliged to spend endless nights in the shelter. As certain events unfolded, the first being the Blitz, we slept there for long periods every night as a matter of course.

It was decided the shelter would be put just on the other side of the fence. My father had already cut out part of the fence, hinged it and put on a handle, and for all I know it is there to this day. It was certainly there when my parents moved out forty years later. My father also built a small lobby on the front of the shelter and ran in electricity to enable us to have light. All in all it was very comfortable when the time came for us to use it regularly.

7

I Want to Go Home

During the first months of the war life seemed to go on as normal, apart from no schooling for the children in London who were not evacuated to safer areas of the country. Mr Sparrow still ran his little 'school', keeping those of us who attended off the streets and occupied.

As we were a mixed group of varying ages and abilities, most of what we did would come under the heading of 'project work'. Having taught in a village school for many years where in one class I had the equivalent of the spectrum of the whole infant school range, I know it is the only way to use the abilities of the entire class at the same time as keeping going their learning of the basic literacy and numeracy skills. It enables each child to feel they are participating in all class enterprises.

In his normal teaching post Mr Sparrow would not, in a London school, have had such a varied age range, and it must be remembered that teaching methods were more formal at that time.

We did a little basic work but we also learned interesting things which, I remember, included a little Greek mythology. We did art work and our acting skills were not neglected. We even did a little gardening.

Mr Sparrow was, I suppose, doing what village school teachers had always had to do – getting the most out of each child. I believe he was rather ahead of his time without being aware of it.

It was many years later, when I read *An Experiment in Education* by Sybil Marshall, that I realised what a success Mr Sparrow had been to occupy us just when it was needed most.

Of course we are all aware that 'project work' has been popular now for many, many years. But I venture to say it must not be at the expense of basic literacy and numeracy; without these, children will flounder no matter how interesting are the projects.

I must also be forthright and add that it still amazes me that so many parents still consider the whole burden of teaching the young to be the responsibility of the teachers in school. So many do not realise that they as parents have the time and opportunity to nurture in their children enquiring minds and an interest in anything and everything that is taking place in the world around them – far and wide and close at hand. No opportunity should be wasted. 'Why' and 'how' are surely two of the most important words which are uttered by children when their intellect is developing.

My father made the most of every opportunity in this respect, and none remains more vivid in my memory than an event which took place one evening between the final days of May 1940 and the first few days of June. This was the week when our army was evacuated from the beaches of Dunkirk in France.

A never-ending stream of over a thousand rescue ships of every shape, size and description, including 220 British naval vessels, sailed to Dunkirk to assist in the transportation of a third of a million troops back to the United Kingdom.

During that eventful week in our history my father arrived home from work one evening and told us to eat our meal quickly, get ourselves 'properly' dressed – always a requisite for a special occasion – because we were going on an important trip.

We travelled by bus to a large railway station in the centre of London, and during the journey Dad was explaining to us the reason for our trip. Being ten years of age at the time of this event, I recall every minute detail of that evening's outing. When we arrived I could not believe there could be so many platforms in one railway station and the spectacle which greeted us will remain with me forever.

There were ladies with urns who were dispensing tea, soup, sandwiches etc. There were hundreds of soldiers, sitting, standing and even lying everywhere. At least my father told me they were soldiers, but to the eye of a ten-year-old girl the sight of the men I saw being disgorged from a train which drew into the station left room for doubt. I actually saw men leave the train and immediately sit or lie down on the platform. They had probably been sleeping on the train and were ready to return to their slumbers without properly waking up in between. Comrades and members of organisations who were on hand to help assisted them to their feet and they all made their way to where we were standing and where refreshments awaited them.

I realised then that they were soldiers. They had on army trousers or army tunics but not always both. Some to this day I will swear had on army trousers and striped pyjama tops or vice versa. Since that time we have all now become familiar with films of the Dunkirk evacuation and we have seen the troops wading through the sea under gunfire to reach the waiting large and small craft. What they were wearing by the time they reached our shores was of little importance.

111

Oh, how grateful I have always been to my father for that evening's experience. But sadly, I cannot remember ever telling him so.

However, there was one mystery surrounding that evening which was not resolved for forty years.

I remembered the front of the station being what I considered rather grand, with wide impressive steps leading up to the entrance. As I have commented, it was a very big station with many platforms. One central London station which I have frequently used while living in Kent is Victoria. As many of the troops landed on the Kent coast, over the years I have been completely bewildered because the front of Victoria Station in no way resembles the front of the station which I have always so vividly remembered.

It was a riddle which could have been solved so easily by asking my father, and why I never did so is a mystery to me. But suddenly, all those years later, all was revealed.

I needed to travel by train to visit a patient who was in St Thomas's Hospital and the nearest railway station with the most convenient train times was Waterloo East. I am certain I never knew of its existence until that time.

When I alighted from the train at Waterloo East and began my short walk to the hospital, I passed the front of Waterloo Station. Lo and behold, there was the entrance which I remembered.

I was indeed fortunate to have a father who considered it important that we see a little bit of our history unfolding that day so long ago.

By the spring of 1940 the schools in London were still not open, but this seems not to have been the case in regard to secondary schools. Although they too were evacuated, some provision had been made to keep them going for the education of children who were not evacuated.

It is remarkable how so many routine procedures continued at that time. There may have been a war in progress, but some things went on uninterrupted and early in 1940 my parents were informed that I had to sit the scholarship examination. My mother accompanied me to a strange school where I recognised no other pupil. I can remember feeling very lonely standing there in a red coat and a large black velour hat.

In due course we were informed that I had been awarded a Junior County Scholarship. It was the summer of 1940.

To this day I have all the relevant letters and documents pertaining to this event in my father's life. I say 'my father's life' because to me at that time it was just correspondence which was helping to decide which senior school I would be attending, but to my father it meant a great deal, hence his retaining the documents for forty years before handing them to me not long before he died.

I find it touching to see his arithmetical workings on the back of the documents. Forms obviously had to be filled in regarding the grant which I received to help with the additional expenses. The education was free but school uniform and other extras, not to mention remaining at school for years after the leaving age of fourteen, must have meant sacrifices on the part of my parents.

As I have already written, I find it touching when I realise that the information required must have been mostly on a yearly basis and my father, who was paid a weekly wage, had painstakingly worked out his yearly salary, mortgage repayments and the rateable value, and even noted the insurance deducted from his weekly wage. His final figure was under his heading 'Income from all sources'.

He even wrote down a few words in various ways, obviously to ensure that his grammar was correct. I wish I had studied these documents and thanked him for preserving them.

From the list of schools which I was sent I chose the Clapton County Secondary School, simply because it was close to my home. My second choice was Skinners' Company School for a very simple reason – I discovered that their blazers were of red and black stripes, which I rather admired. Fortunately I was accepted by my first choice, which we always called the John Howard School. Some years later after various changes in our educational system it did become the John Howard Secondary School.

Many secondary schools were named after important people in our history. In Canterbury we have the Simon Langton Grammar Schools named after an Archbishop of Canterbury and in nearby Folkestone the grammar schools have the name William Harvey, the physician who discovered the circulation of the blood.

John Howard was a prison reformer who was born in Clapton, Hackney, in 1726, the son of a prosperous middle-class family. Although a Non-conformist he was appointed High Sheriff of Bedfordshire and was responsible for the county gaol, where the conditions and human degradation appalled him.

During the mid 1750s many gaols held religious dissenters and debtors as well as common thieves and other criminals. The former were quite often respectable local persons, often tradesmen who could not be released from prison until money was raised to pay off their creditors.

John Howard was critical of what he saw in Bedford gaol. As the original purpose of Sheriff of Bedfordshire was to ensure the safety of the judge, and hundreds of years had gone by since a judge was kidnapped, it gave John Howard plenty of time to spend in court and he soon noticed that although not guilty, prisoners were still taken back to gaol until they paid the gaoler's fee, the reason being that the gaoler received no salary and depended on these fees for his livelihood. John Howard decided to tour other English counties, hoping to find an example for Bedford gaol to follow.

He was allowed to visit cells, dungeons, even torture chambers, and talked to gaolers and prisoners, only to find to his horror that what he had seen in Bedford was common all over England and Wales. He then felt compelled to visit Ireland and Scotland and eventually toured Europe and Russia.

This was at a time when travel was dangerous and usually uncomfortable. He travelled thousands of miles on horseback and spent some £30,000, which is estimated at about £500,000 today, of his own money, determined to improve prison conditions. He entered prisons in disguise in defiance of governments who feared the power of his writings. He made seven large-scale journeys between 1775 and 1790, the first two of these are described in his book.

The importance of his life and work in the development of the international penal reform movement is reflected on this inscription on his statue in St Paul's Cathedral:

> This extraordinary man had the fortune
>   To be honoured whilst living,
> In the manner which his virtues deserved:
>   He received the thanks
> Of both houses of the British and Irish parliaments,
> For his eminent services rendered to his country
>   and to mankind.

His work at Bedford made him known in his own country but the publication of his book made him an authority on prison matters in Europe. By personal initiatives he aroused the consciences of many influential persons and stirred them into action.

Late in 1789 he set off once more for Eastern Europe. After tending to a prisoner with typhus at Kherson in the

Ukraine he became ill and died of typhus in January 1790 at the age of sixty-four. He was buried in Russia and a monument was erected there to mark his life and achievements.

I am proud to think my school had a link with this great man, albeit only by name. It was nice to know his good works were recognised and I am a little sad that the school is now called a technology college without the prefix John Howard, for I am certain he would have approved of the educational advances which have been made since his time.

And so I began to look forward to my new school. A great fuss had been made of my scholarship by family and friends. I had a party for six of my friends and have a photograph of us having tea in the garden. This may not sound terribly exciting but until that day parties had been only family gatherings and this was something special. I was also taken shopping by my father to buy a present. I chose a manicure set in a morocco leather box. I thought it was beautiful with its bevelled mirror set in the lid.

Perhaps it was having this gift that made me 'nail conscious'. I was attending Sunday school when I noticed an older girl was wearing nail varnish, the colour of which took my eye. When I admired it she offered me what was left in the bottle for the princely sum of threepence. I was never given pocket money but somehow acquired the threepence – probably sweet money. The following Sunday I gave her the threepence but never received the nail varnish, and never forgot the incident or the colour of the nail varnish which was called 'light rust'. The fact that I would never have been allowed to wear it obviously never entered my head.

Things rapidly progressed in preparation for my new school venture. Considering the state of affairs nationally, everything associated with my education seemed to be going smoothly.

Although the school was evacuated, the headmistress interviewed the new pupils and parents at the school. I was accompanied by my mother. After the interview we were taken to be measured for our school uniforms, which were supplied by an outfitters in Leicester. It was a very attractive brown and cream uniform, different in many ways to most school's. The blouse was collarless with a square neck and the tunic had side pleats with a buttoned belt. Most other uniforms had a tie and a knotted sash. Our hat and blazer badges and the cord around the blazer were of our house colour: green, yellow, red, blue or purple. Mine was unfortunately Rome house and the colour was purple. I am told by a friend that other schools referred to us as the 'brown girls'. Not surprising, as even our stockings were brown, described in the uniform price list as tan lisle, price three shillings and sixpence. The only part of the uniform which was not popular was the gymnasium attire, also dark brown and resembling a cotton one-piece sleeveless bathing costume. It is an understatement to say it was not glamorous, but it was functional. For myself it mattered little, I was physically very immature, but the more developed girls hated them. The price list for all of these 'Uniform Garments', as it is headed, makes for interesting reading.

And so I was kitted out ready for the first day of school. Not the most desirable time for starting out on a new venture. The summer of 1940 had begun with the Dunkirk episode, followed by the Battle of Britain and the Blitz. The bombing of London had a considerable effect on our way of life and it was at its height when I was due to begin school.

*

Although I have always been of the opinion that I was rather cosseted as a child, like most children I was not accompanied by my mother every time I ventured out on to the streets. And the day I set off for my new school I was alone. Otherwise, doubtless my mother would have noticed something amiss when I arrived at the school.

The school day had only just begun when I realised that I was dressed entirely in brown while every other girl was in green.

I was very quickly taken to the headmistress's study, where it was explained to me that my school was not using its own school premises. The building had been taken over by the North Hackney Central School. I do not remember why this was, but it had something to do with the war. Maybe their school had been damaged during an air-raid. Whatever the reason, I stuck out like a sore thumb and I must have been close to tears all day. Not a nice experience for any child.

I was given a letter to take home which explained all. Somehow a letter informing my parents of the change of location for my first day of school had gone astray. Not surprising, with the Blitz in full swing.

My school, like most others in London, was evacuated, but for pupils who did not wish to be evacuated provision had been made.

Dalston County Secondary School were the proud owners of a new building. To describe it as a lovely building with excellent educational facilities does not do it justice. That it had been built in the 1930s was obviously the reason for the Art Deco influence. The main staircase was a huge curved marble feature with a black wrought-iron balustrade and balusters.

Other features of the school were just as impressive. Unlike most school assembly halls, which are equipped with wall bars covering the walls for use when the hall is used as a gymnasium, this hall was very large and the stage accommodated a grand piano. Underneath the stage was the green room.

The gymnasium was situated elsewhere and had changing rooms and showers. How I hated having a shower – I still dislike them.

The library was not furnished with the usual school chairs but with chairs and armchairs upholstered in brown leather. What luxury in a school.

As well as the usual outdoor sports facilities there was a beautiful rose garden, consisting of a centre lawn with a bed of roses in each corner, surrounded on three sides by the school buildings.

Many of the classrooms overlooked this picturesque view and we sometimes found it a distraction when a lesson was in progress. I consider myself extremely fortunate and privileged to have had my first experience of serious education in such surroundings.

Until the summer of 1943 this school was temporarily renamed the N.E. London Emergency Secondary School for Girls. The headmistress of the Dalston County School was its headmistress, but the staff contained mistresses from all the schools which made up this emergency school.

What an assortment of uniforms there were, each school strictly preserving their own identity. Looking back, it is easy to see why we as a school were called the 'brown girls' because most of the other school uniforms were primarily black or navy blue. We were also different in that we were kept together as a group and not split up into different forms because our first foreign language was German. This was very unusual; most, if not all, the other schools began with French. It was a number of years later when I queried the reason for this that I was given the explanation that most of the fee-paying pupils were Jewish (of this I was already aware). I was told, 'He who pays the piper calls the tune. German is akin to Yiddish.' Another riddle solved.

Back to my first day at school. I arrived home with my letter from the Central School headmistress. When my father arrived back from work it was decided we must set out to find this emergency school in Dalston. It seems strange that we could not enquire of any other parents in the same situation, but there was no other girl to our knowledge who was a pupil at my school. With our uniform we were hardly inconspicuous, and we would have noticed any girl attired in it.

Mum, Dad, my brother and I set off and, after walking just over one mile, Hackney Downs was reached. This suddenly was not our district and it is an example of how parochial London was at that time. We were venturing into a different borough. On this outward journey we took the road running along the side of the park and made our way until we eventually found the school.

Having found it, we did an about-turn and started on our return journey. This time we went through Hackney Downs and sat on a park bench for a little rest and to discuss the issue. It must be remembered that at that time the Blitz was at its height and we were aware that we would be spending that night sleeping in the shelter. Both my parents were anxious to reach home before the air-raid siren sounded – not that we waited for that signal before going to the shelter. Oh no, we settled down regularly every night to avoid having to get out of bed and make the trip in the middle of the night.

To this day I can remember the 'discussion' which took place on that park bench. It was, to put it mildly, a little more heated than a discussion.

There was no way that I could go by bus to the school This would have entailed so much walking at each end of the bus journey that it would not have benefited me. However, to walk all the way with an air raid often in progress was, in my mother's opinion, absolutely unthinkable. But my father was adamant. I have recorded before that education to him was the be-all and end-all, and he was determined that I should benefit from the place offered me.

That he won the day was the best outcome there could have been to the situation, and the next day I was taken to the school, where I was pleased to meet up with other 'brown girls'.

One would think by the age of eleven and in the wake of various episodes in my short life, I would have realised that I did not like being away from home and family. But I obviously never learned, and after a few days I begged my parents to allow me to be evacuated to Bishops Stortford, where my real school was sharing the premises of the girls' high school.

My parents gave in under pressure and we all set off for Bishops Stortford. We visited the school, met my headmistress, Dr Hunt, once again, and were given the address of a family who were ready to put me up. They had one daughter, who was about my age. My sleeping accommodation was rather strange but this was war-time and at home I would have been sleeping in an iron half-buried hut in the garden – the Anderson shelter. The space under the staircase was high in the front – the door having been removed – and the ceiling sloped down at the back to the floor, but there was room for a mattress on the floor and the front of this cupboard/room faced the kitchen. It was not horribly closed in, just rather strange as a bedroom.

We went shopping and my mother bought me a new jumper and promised to make me a skirt to match it when she returned home. I was also given writing paper, envelopes and stamps, which was just as well, considering how the week progressed.

The next day was Saturday and I settled down to write to Auntie Nellie and my grandmother. The post must have been very efficient even during the war, for within a few days I had received a letter and a postal order from each. Early the following week I also received a parcel from home. It contained the skirt promised by my mother and made during the weekend, something from my brother, but I do not recall what this was, and some pieces of shrapnel which my father had promised to find for the little girl with whom I was billeted.

On the Sunday I heard on the radio a broadcast from London and in the background I heard the air-raid siren sound followed by gunfire in the distance. I wanted to go home. I immediately set about writing to request my return to London. This being my only means of communication, I wrote every day. I talked to my form-mistress, who sent me to the headmistress, to whom I repeated continually, 'I want to go home,' I cried the whole time. I recall one day combing my hair in front of a mirror and being terribly upset because through my tears I was unable to see my reflection well enough to get a straight centre parting in my hair.

Even the lady in the post office took pity on me. I had used all my writing paper and went to buy more. The assistant very kindly gave me paper, envelope and stamp – and off went another letter.

On the Thursday of that week as I came out of school – jubilation – I saw my young brother in the distance and I realised salvation was at hand. My mother and he had come to take me home. Many years later my mother told me that she had visited the school that day and had spoken to Dr Hunt, who had informed her that home-sickness was quite common and the girls usually got over it, but in my case she advised my mother to take me home before I made myself ill with fretting.

And so I was taken home and returned to the emergency school, where we were to remain for the next three years, until our own school returned from evacuation.

During the few days that I was away my mother had discovered that a few hundred yards away there was another girl who, like me, had just become a 'brown girl'. She was the daughter of the fire chief and the family lived above the fire station. I became quite friendly with her and visited her home quite often, when we would sit out in the garden, which was situated on the roof. It was a very unusual and attractive setting.

As the Blitz was still at its height, often in the morning the girl's father would send his car to pick me up and we would be transported to school in style.

Within a few days I discovered a few girls lived about a mile from my home and we began to meet up and continue the journey to school together. One girl's father worked some nights in Fleet Street on a newspaper, and if he came home in the morning from night-work he would accompany us to school before going home to rest.

My father had bought our house two years before the war and by the time my grandmother moved out, enabling us to have use of the whole house, the war was almost upon us. He had decorated the vacated rooms downstairs and we were using the kitchen-cum-living-room and the front sitting-room which were furnished, but the centre room, meant to be a dining room, was empty. So, when the Blitz took its toll on the bedrooms upstairs – only superficial damage, broken windows etc. – it was decided to bring down the beds into the unused room for the nights when we did not have to sleep in the air-raid shelter. But for some time, as I have said, we regularly slept in the shelter rather than be disturbed in the middle of the night.

The baker and his wife joined us every night in the shelter, as was the arrangement when it was put in their garden. Their two boys had been sent out of London when the bombing became heavy, but with only the six of us it was still a little cramped. Even more so when the owner of the post office asked if she could share the accommodation with us. Fortunately, she only did this for a few weeks, because she was rather a stout elderly lady and in her fur coat she took up an enormous amount of space. She must have found an alternative answer to her problem – probably a Morrison shelter in the house. This was a reinforced table-like structure under which one would sleep for some protection.

Every morning my young brother would help carry the blankets etc. belonging to the baker up the garden to his premises, and his wife would take my brother into the shop and let him choose a pastry. We would watch him scanning the window selection, all aware that his eyes would finally alight on, and he would point to, a madeleine.

Everything sold in the baker's was made and baked on the premises. To accomplish all this work, the baker would rise at four o'clock in the morning and commence his day. Shelter life did not really fit in with his sleeping needs and one day he decided, with the assistance of my father, to strengthen his cellar and sleep down there. But in the middle of the night he heard dreadful bangs and explosions outside his shop. He said he heard commands being given. Whether or not small anti-aircraft guns actually moved around the streets of London at the height of the Blitz I know not, but he certainly returned to the shelter very swiftly that night.

Whether his premises were blasted during the bombing in any way I cannot remember. I believe not, but he closed

124

his business and moved away to the country. I missed seeing him take out the bread from the ovens and making those delicious pastries. And we could no longer run down his garden to buy freshly baked hot-cross buns.

The Blitz continued and we gradually got used to it, becoming quite blasé about it in many ways. For instance, the cinema visits. If the management showed on the screen that an air raid was in progress, we would leave the cinema and return home. But after a little while we ceased to react in this way. It would be shown on the screen that the air-raid siren had sounded and we would hear anti-aircraft gunfire accompanying the film soundtrack, but we continued to watch the film. This attitude continued for the remaining five years we were at war.

We became accustomed to going out in the dark holding a small torch to assist our journey, particularly shining it to show the edge of the pavement when crossing the road, for there were no street lights or lights shining from windows. The blackout was rigidly enforced. And as Number 8 batteries were needed for these small torches, they joined the ever-growing list of 'items which were in short supply'. Along with other little luxuries such as bananas, if a shop had some to sell, a queue would form and we children would be sent to join it until our mothers could take our place.

Although visits to the cinema were to continue regularly as our principal form of entertainment, some things did change as a consequence of the Blitz. Regular excursions to the heart of London with my father on Sunday mornings – tram journeys and visits to well-known sights and monuments. Not only the largest edifices but Cleopatra's Needle, Boadicea riding her chariot and feeding the pigeons in Trafalgar Square. All came to an end. So too did the Sunday lunch routine with my grandparents. They thought it best that I did not visit them during the Blitz and I never resumed the practice again.

With the baker and his wife now moved away, we four had the shelter to ourselves. But not for long.

An aunt, uncle and cousin became victims of a parachute mine; their house was completely destroyed and not a stick of furniture remained. Fortunately, the occupants were in the Anderson shelter. They immediately came to live with us, occupying our front sitting-room.

Our shelter was enlarged and once again made very comfortable by my father's efforts. It still had the little entrance porch, which my father considered an extra precaution against blast, the door being at a right angle to the shelter entrance, and we still had electric light and radio. It didn't take long for the earth which had been excavated to accommodate the shelter, and with which the shelter had been covered, to produce abundant foliage – I suspect with some assistance from Dad, who loved gardening.

I am reminded of a little story which happened one year after the war. My young brother, about eleven years of age at the time, acquired, I know not how, a baby goat. This little kid was adorable, not much larger than a newborn baby lamb. It had plenty of room to play, because the baker when he left allowed us free use of his garden and my father also kept an eye on the baker's vacated premises. I think the goat was called Billy, not very original, and he was fed from a bottle. I remember being greatly put out one Saturday evening when my parents and brother had already left for the cinema and the baby goat required his bottle of milk. I prepared it and set about feeding him, but he was so excited I was showered with milk. As I was all dressed ready to go to a dance, I was not happy. But that little goat during the time it was with us completely cleared the old air-raid shelter of its lush green covering.

Back to 1940. Our live-in relatives were really welcomed by me because my cousin was the closest to my age in the family. She was one year younger than me and we were good friends. It meant that we could enjoy each other's company in the shelter, as we often had to go to there early in the evening.

Like most young girls, we were always being 'told off' for giggling and acting silly, but one night I remember we were very sombre. We had been to the cinema and seen a film called *Geronimo*. The scalping practised by the Indians had terrified us and when we settled down to sleep that night my cousin, whose bunk was across the rear of the shelter, had her pillow, blankets etc. changed around to enable us to hold hands when we went to sleep. My bunk being down the side of the shelter, we were also able to sleep heads close together.

I know not whether that film made as great an impression on her as it did me, but it was a few years before I would consider going to see a film which had any other than a 'U' rating. I believe an 'A' rating meant that a child could see the film if accompanied by an adult. Not this child – it caused a few altercations but I was adamant.

As I have already recorded in this narrative, visits to the doctor were very rare, but our parents had their little remedies which would be produced when necessary. On two occasions I recall my father doing just that.

The first was during the night of Sunday September 8th 1940. Berger, the paint manufacturers, were situated a few hundred yards from my home. On instructions from the government, in 1939 the firm had partly turned over to war production. One day, the warning went just before five o'clock in the evening and a large formation raid over the docks was witnessed. Two gentlemen from Berger decided that their spotting posts at Berger were in a very vulnerable position and, had such a raid taken place locally, their fire watchers would not have stood a chance. A change would have to be implemented immediately.

Fortunately, this was carried out, for the same evening the factory had an extremely narrow escape when a high-explosive bomb skimmed the main gates but luckily fell into open ground. But that luck was not to last. Within twenty-four hours, at 11.10 p.m. on Sunday September 8th, a high explosive bomb or an oil bomb – it was felt that it was probably the latter – fell as a direct hit right in the centre of the varnish storage tank rooms, which contained over 100,000 gallons of varnish, together with a few thousand gallons of other flammable materials.

The local fire brigade obviously needed outside help and this was forthcoming. Over a hundred pumps were used and it took eight hours to extinguish the fire.

It remains very vivid in my memory sixty years on. We were woken by my father and all stood outside the shelter. To our right was this fire, so huge, high and intense that the block of five-storey-high flats opposite my house was lit up so well that it was possible to see the colour of the curtains in each window. There were fire engines everywhere and hoses running along the pavements.

When my father spoke to a fireman he was told that they and the air-raid wardens had done their best to evacuate everyone from their homes in nearby streets. It could not have been an easy operation with so many people not in their houses but in shelters. In our case, the helpers were not aware that our shelter was in the baker's garden.

Not much sleep was had that night, so my father's medicinal expertise was put into operation. Kill or cure is the apt maxim, I believe. I remember the names which were sal volatile and quinine, and I can only assume we sniffed one and swallowed the other. That night was a very nasty experience, even without the bitter medicine.

The Blitz went on for some considerable time and the results of many night and day raids were extremely unpleasant, but during the day life went on as usual and at night we slept comfortably and soundly, particularly we children. We all know that if children are physically comfortable and mentally comfortable, feeling secure and safe (we were in a shelter), not a lot will keep them awake.

I ponder often on this question of children coping now, when so many families are breaking up. I feel particularly strongly about this because, as this narrative has shown, I was so fortunate to have the stability of a home life to which I always knew I could return. Home was always the same, it never changed. There was never a parent missing at night or even at a meal-time.

The second time that I recall our slumbers being particularly disturbed, other than by the usual gunfire or exploding bombs, was when we were all awakened by the most horrendous noise in our shelter. It was actually on the top of the shelter, and we were all terrified.

When Dad went out to investigate, it was nothing more sinister than one of the cables attached to a barrage balloon. These were large balloons, shaped rather like a fat fish. In these days of peace we see a smaller version quite often up aloft, advertising an event taking place. But the one which caused us to panic was the large type used during the war as an obstacle to low-flying enemy aircraft. They were anchored by extremely thick metal cables. One of these barrage balloons had become unanchored and was floating around trailing the metal cables, one of which was scouring the top of our air-raid shelter.

The balloon must have been somewhat deflated because it was bouncing over the roof-tops. We watched it – it was rather a sinister, creepy sight, the balloon was so large.

My father heard the next day that it had eventually landed on the railway track a couple of hundred yards away, and somehow it was disposed of.

That was the second time my father dispensed something to calm us. When I think about how accustomed we had become to gunfire and explosions, it seems strange that we should have been so frightened by such a triviality. But the metal cable had reached the metal of the shelter as it scraped off the earth covering, and to this day I remember the noise being particularly scary because we had been awakened from a deep sleep and in the confines of the shelter the sound was terrifying.

When my father talked of it the next day, he reminded me of the day we had spent on the Hackney Marshes looking at a display of what I can only assume was defence equipment. This event must have taken place at the beginning of the war or even just before, in preparation for the forthcoming hostilities. Whichever, I remember it included a barrage balloon and during my father's detailed description of the balloon and its use, the thickness of the cable had intrigued me – and it certainly helped me to understand the reason for the previous night's scare.

The Hackney Marshes were, and still are, a very large area of open space. At the end which meets the main road it has on one side the River Lea, in which small boys would often be seen swimming. To reach the open fields at this point there were steps leading down from the pavement. It was quite a long flight of steps and the trees growing at the edge

130

of the field were not very much higher than the pavement and main road.

But this is my memory of the field as it was when I was a child. My father told me once that it was infilled and flattened, using the debris from the aftermath of the London Blitz to make it nearer to the level of the pavement. I have not been able to confirm this, but recently I was told that children at that time were not allowed to engage in their favourite pastime of looking for 'treasures' there. This appears to substantiate what my father said regarding the infill.

The Hackney Marshes certainly are an extremely large open space in what is a highly populated part of London. Driving past at the weekend, one can see numerous games of football in action stretching far into the distance.

Not surprisingly, they were chosen as the location for a 'bomb cemetery' during the Second World War, as they were far enough away from inhabited areas for controlled detonations to take place.

I recall once being sent by my mother on an errand. I was walking along the high road when a policemen picked me up and practically threw me into a shop as a vehicle went racing along the road, ringing its bell very loudly. The policeman explained to me that they were taking an unexploded bomb to the Hackney Marshes, which were about half a mile away.

One quite famous event was when a lieutenant and a sapper were each awarded the George Cross for recovering an unexploded bomb from St Paul's Cathedral, removing it to Hackney Marshes, and safely detonating it there.

One very sad story, which alas I am unable to confirm, was an accident which occurred on a Sunday morning. My father, with my very young brother, was walking along the high road which crosses the Hackney Marshes. They were in all probability making their way to the Eton Manor sports ground, namely the Wilderness, when there was an explosion. Dad immediately put my brother in the charge of another pedestrian and raced over to the source of the explosion. The sight which met his eyes was not a pretty one and he ran as fast as he could to the Hackney Hospital, which was only about a quarter of a mile away, to report the accident.

I cannot remember, and probably never knew, how the emergency services were alerted – whether at the hospital by my father, or by my father or another member of the public dialling 999. There were no mobile phones in those days and very few households possessed a private telephone. The call would have to have been made from a public call-box.

The accident occurred during the detonating of a bomb, and when my father returned home he was visibly shaken.

8

I Want to Go Home

My first few months at the new school were rather hectic. Adapting to a completely new routine and making new friends was unsettling enough without the accompaniment of the Blitz going on continually. I had a quick wash and breakfast in the house after sleeping in the shelter, and then went off on the thirty-to-forty-minute walk to school.

A few of us would meet up and complete the journey together, eyes down, looking for shrapnel from raids of the previous nights, which I would collect for my brother.

In the London streets there were small brick air-raid shelters built for passers-by in emergencies. When the anti-aircraft guns were firing, we girls would take cover in a shelter. I think it was more for the fun than for the safety aspect, and it produced lots of laughter and giggles. Even by myself I would occasionally enter one of these shelters if necessary. I am certain that I would not feel happy about a child doing such a thing in this day and age, but children seemed to be safer in those days, if one forgets the bombing factor.

As I have already recorded, we became accustomed to the bombing, but it took a few weeks for me to come to terms with being away from home when an air raid was in progress and one could hear anti-aircraft fire and the occasional explosion. What a wimp I must have seemed.

The heaviest daylight raids were from the first week of

September to the first week of October, which was the first month I attended the new school. On the September 15th the Germans made a supreme effort which proved to be the climax of their daylight raids and the most triumphant day of all for the RAF. The enemy were then constrained to try to achieve their object by night raids, although the day raids did not cease completely.

It was during the first couple of weeks, when day raids were most frequent, that my weakness was exposed yet again.

On two or three occasions the air-raid siren was heard and our form made its way to the cloakrooms, which may have been in the basement or only on the ground floor – I cannot remember which, only that that was the drill if an air raid was in progress.

The rest of the form may have made its way there but not I. I, on these two or three occasions, put on my hat and blazer and set off for home. I walked and ran as fast as my little legs would carry me. Nothing slowed down my journey back. The 'I want to go home' scenario was rearing its ugly head again.

As part of my school uniform I was obliged to wear brown stockings. These were kept up by suspenders, which were a definite necessity in my case because, to put it nicely, my legs were rather slim.

In my hurry to reach home, first one suspender and then another would become undone, and by the time I reached home I would be lucky if any of the four were still attached to my stockings. I would not stop running to rectify the situation, that would have slowed me down, and in any case it was hardly the kind of thing one did in public. By the time I reached home my mother would open the front door to find me standing there trying desperately to keep up my stockings by clutching tunic and a stocking in each hand,

134

and at the same time trying to juggle with my music case containing school books; we never used satchels.

This has changed greatly over the years and one sees children, often quite small children, walking to and from school with laden satchels. Apparently pupils do not always have a desk of their own in school in which to keep all their books. They certainly seem to carry around far more than we did. We only took home what was necessary for that evening's homework.

Back to my misdemeanours. I cannot recall my mother being terribly angry with me at the time, which would have been understandable under the circumstances. She was capable of being extremely angry when occasions arose but she must have understood what motivated me to take such drastic action as to run home during the school day. This was at a time when the school day meant a day spent at school. Nobody left the premises at lunch-time unless they lived close enough to go home for lunch, and very few of us were that fortunate. You were not allowed to leave early; any free periods were spent in the library. We were not even allowed time at home to revise for exams.

Now when the pupils' examinations are taking place they spend a great deal of their time at home revising, attending school only when necessary to sit an examination. And when the exams are over they often do not return to school to complete the term.

Not so when we were pupils. I remember a very unusual event which took place involving my friend and me and the biology lab skeleton. The episode is not easily forgotten.

When we had been attending the North East London Emergency Secondary School for three years, our own school, Clapton County, returned from Bishops Stortford to settle once again in its own premises. I assume the other schools with whom we had been sharing the emergency school returned also from evacuation and Dalston County regained their beautiful school to themselves.

It was quite a culture shock to be taken from the splendour of that school to our own establishment. This was a very old building, but it had character and we were all very proud of it.

In the front reception area was The Oak Staircase, which we girls were not allowed to use. Not that any of us would have been that keen to do so, for at the top of the staircase was Dr Hunt's study. Attitudes may have changed in recent years but I can assure readers that we had no great desire to encounter the headmistress unnecessarily, albeit she was a superb headmistress and a very kind and understanding lady, as demonstrated when she advised my mother to take me home when I tried my hand at being evacuated.

However, I digress. Back to the skeleton.

We had finished our examinations and were due to leave school a few weeks later. Our time at school completed, there was no reason to revise or study for any specific reason and we were a little bored. Not being allowed to leave the premises, we had to fill our time somehow. One day my friend and I had an idea. We were both fond of art and thought it would be a worthwhile activity to make drawings of the biology laboratory skeleton, if we were allowed to move it, the biology lab being situated on the ground floor and the art room on the first floor.

We were given permission and set about our task. The skeleton was housed in a tall, narrow box, the front of which was the door. When one opened the door of this receptacle there, suspended on a hook from the top of the box, was the complete skeleton of, we always believed, a fifteen-year-old girl. Whether that was true or not really doesn't matter, but it was quite awesome and was the cause of many gasps, shrieks and giggles when we confronted new entrants to the school with the container and requested them to open its door.

On the day chosen to practise our artistic skills, my friend and I unhooked the skeleton and, holding it aloft somehow by the large hook from which it hung, we very gingerly moved it from the biology department to the art room.

When we had completed our drawings we had the ominous task of returning it to the box in the lab.

Rebellious by nature my friend and I definitely were not. Perhaps we were feeling rather daring because we were leaving school. For whatever reason we, who were normally very sensible young ladies, decided to 'chance our luck', which I believe is the correct expression under the circumstances, and take the skeleton home via The Oak Staircase.

We got as far as the turn of the staircase, where I believe there was a small area where we were able to rest. Unfortunately, by that time silliness got the better of us and we began to giggle. The skeleton began to sway from the hook which one of us was holding. Various parts of it were hooked together and it does not require much imagination to picture what happened next. A couple of pieces of the skeleton fell to the floor. Not just to the floor – oh no – they clattered down The Oak Staircase.

What a noise! The headmistress, whose study was at the top of the staircase, came hot foot from her room, peered over the top and must have been so amazed at what she saw that she was almost speechless. I cannot remember exactly what she said, but had we not been on the point of leaving I am certain we would have been more severely reprimanded, if not expelled.

The little story just narrated came about because we were not allowed to leave school when our examinations were completed and certainly not just because an air raid was in progress – to which I will now return.

I must have been scolded in a mild manner by my mother for returning from school without permission, but it was definitely never referred to at school. I therefore am quite certain that Mum must have visited the school and had an interview with the headmistress. Taking everything into account, those few weeks were an unusual, difficult time for everyone and the less fuss made about my problem in the hope that it would just fade away in time was without doubt the correct approach. The problem did fade away, helped no doubt by daylight raids becoming far less frequent.

Today we appear to be more aware of children's problems but do we not make big issues out of what are quite often minor problems? We all know there are children with severe behavioural difficulties but as an ex-primary school teacher I question whether the educational psychologist needs to be called upon quite so soon as he or she often is. Children have always had their 'difficult' periods, but with discipline and love most of the time the problems were resolved.

I taught at my last school for ten years. It was a village school with only three teachers, the infant class of fives-to-sevens being in my charge. There were never more than seventy children in the school and my class never exceeded twenty-three in number.

Many people will say that with only that number of children in a class, behavioural problems should be easier to deal with. But I can assure those persons that the problems of a small class, which is made up of an age range which in a larger school will be perhaps in four separate classes, are just as many if not more than those of a larger class of children all of the same age whose stages of mental and physical development will not be as diverse.

In the school just mentioned, the two teachers of the sevens-to-nines and nines-to-elevens had the same problems with such a large age range as myself, but in the ten years I taught there I cannot recall any behavioural problems which necessitated our calling in additional help from the services which were available.

It may not be a popular belief but nevertheless it is a fact that without discipline and rules relating to what is and what is not acceptable behaviour, the classroom situation can become intolerable and the more reticent child will be intimidated by the bully, who will be victorious.

The time when a teacher of young children could treat those in her charge as she would her own offspring has long gone.

People who are anti the occasional smack on the legs of a child who has been exceptionally naughty always talk about 'beating', which is rather an extreme description for a slap given at the moment when a child has overstepped the boundary in a physical way. But this kind of situation in my experience was so rare as to be practically non-existent. A good reprimand and the firm placing of the wrongdoer on a chair from which he or she would not dare to move usually sufficed. In fact I have never known it not to work, perhaps because they knew that they had done wrong and that they would be forgiven. After five or ten minutes of being ignored – time for him or her to calm down – I would beckon the child over, sit him on my lap, put my arm around him and say something like, 'So! What has upset you this morning, sunshine?'

All was resolved, no hard feelings. I like to think that we teachers were firm but kind. The children knew where to run to when they were in trouble: straight to the teacher, who would give them a hug, sympathise with them, plant a kiss with their fingers on a grazed knee. After all, a teacher is standing in for the parent.

All these actions are taken spontaneously and decisively and in my opinion make more sense than kneeling down and having an in-depth conversation with a six-year-old, while the rest of the class think you are not aware of them and therefore decide to be disruptive.

But I am afraid I am being nostalgic. Those times are not likely to return. I am told one is not allowed now to smack a pupil and sitting a child on one's knee and giving him a hug is definitely not allowed. The children seem to me to be the losers. To whom do they turn when they need a little reassurance and guidance?

I will never change my opinion that with more discipline, kindness and understanding from a very early age there would be less need for child psychologists and counsellors.

I have strayed a long way from the story of my running home from school two or three times when the air-raid siren sounded, but I hope I have put over the point that often plenty of common-sense and as little fuss as possible goes a long way to solving many problems when dealing with children.

I settled into my new school very nicely and among my new friends were girls who were to remain my friends for life. Unfortunately, I no longer socialised with my old friends. We did not attend the same schools and we completely lost touch although we lived in close proximity.

I suppose it began with homework. This was probably the most important difference between us. It is difficult to expect the readers of this narrative to understand in an age when every child has a secondary education of one kind or another, albeit some will have more emphasis put on academic subjects than others.

My original school friends remained at elementary school until the age of fourteen and then left to begin earning their living. Two, however, went to what was called a 'central school', where the emphasis appears to have been on what were then known as 'commercial subjects', which included shorthand, typing, book-keeping etc. These subjects were not in our curriculum but could be studied in the sixth form if so desired.

The 'central schools' were also sometimes referred to as 'technical schools', particularly those which were for boys. It is a name which continued to be used for many years and is self-explanatory in its description of the subjects taught. But my school was academic, culminating in the taking of the School Certificate examination after five years and the Higher School Certificate after a further two years. The latter, like 'A' levels, was the road to university or teacher training college.

At the end of the Second World War a new Education Act came into operation. It provided free secondary education for every child. The term 'elementary education' no longer existed. Education until the age of eleven was called 'primary education', which included nursery, infant and junior ages.

The 'Eleven Plus' examination came into being, and children then attended a grammar school, which was what my school became, for academic training, a technical school or a secondary modern school.

Whereas in my day one talked of 'winning a scholarship', the 'Eleven Plus' produced the horrid term 'failing the Eleven Plus', which was unfortunate because it was a test simply to ensure that children would benefit from the secondary education best suited to their abilities.

I was certainly very happy with the type of school chosen for me and I began to enjoy every new experience which it offered.

The German mistress was our particular friend. She was a member of staff of our own school because, as I have already written, we were unusual in that German was our

141

principal foreign language. She really was great fun and tolerated our rather naughty behaviour in the first year very well. I think she realised it was a rather difficult time for everybody. But I cannot remember any of us being the slightest bit naughty with any other mistress and the German mistress remained our very good friend the whole of our time at school. A few of us offered to help her with her gardening chores when we left school, but we never did.

Another teacher who was extremely bountiful with her kindness and time was the music mistress. She was very young and very pretty. One day a few of us were looking through her music, which was on the piano. Being inquisitive is second nature to eleven-year-olds. We were actually not looking for anything in particular, but hopeful that we might find a piece of music which appealed to us. She was always willing to play music at our request.

We were in luck in two respects. The first was in discovering her age. She was twenty-four years old. This was deduced by the inscription on the inside cover of a book of music. Why do young pupils obtain so much pleasure and feel so important from discovering something so trivial with regard to a teacher? But it is so. We felt very important with our secret knowledge.

Our second piece of luck that day was finding among the music the piano solo of the *Warsaw Concerto*. This was a real 'find' It was composed by Richard Addinsell and featured in the very popular film at that time called *Dangerous Moonlight*. It was a piece of music which had become very popular and when we found the music on the piano we were overjoyed.

As already stated, the music mistress was very generous with her time, and day after day when we had finished our lunch a few of us would gather in the hall and settle down to listen to her rendering of this wonderful music.

One day this mistress married, and at the suggestion of

the headmistress we all subscribed to her wedding present by placing our pennies all the way around the hall. The headmistress attended the wedding and described her as a beautiful billowing cloud of white, floating down the aisle.

I know from my professional experience that a teacher can both make or break a child's enthusiasm, they wield a great deal of power, which can be beneficial or detrimental to that enthusiasm. I always met with encouragement, first in infant school then junior shool, and in secondary school it continued.

I was still playing the piano at home by the tonic sol-fa method. The Sunday newspaper which my father bought also printed quite a number of the words and music of popular songs of the time. Because they also included the tonic sol-fa, I would cut them out, stick them on cardboard and decorate them. I had quite a collection.

One of the first songs we learned with our friendly music mistress had, I observed, tonic sol-fa as well as music on my copy. I asked if I might take it home to copy the words and the tonic sol-fa, and she not only allowed me to do this but always made a point of lending me the book or sheet music of any song which we were learning to enable me to copy it. I still have the book containing these 'musical' efforts. It was to be a year before my mother found a music teacher willing to give me music lessons, but that young music mistress had kept my interest alive during that year with her understanding and encouragement.

I am finding it difficult to explain the whole new world which seemed to be opening up to me at that time. I was meeting people and learning about things in a way which was completely new to me. Thanks to my father, I had been used to ferreting out knowledge for myself, and now it seemed I had like-minded classmates and members of staff, and learning was interesting and also fun.

In junior school we had listened to programmes for

143

schools on the radio but visual aids were non-existent. There was no television, there were no videos. But good drama was always available in London and we were fortunate in seeing Shakespeare performed by superb actors. We were not always the audience, we also participated in many plays during our time at secondary school, not only as modules of English lessons but also part of our German and history lessons. The form once even endeavoured to write a play about Joan of Arc but I cannot remember it ever coming to fruition.

The first history mistress we had was, I am certain, way ahead of her time in her approach to the subject. During our first winter at school, we had begun way back in the annals of English history and must have reached the village system which was prevalent in England during Saxon times. It so happened that we had a lot of snow at the time. How long the snow lasted I know not, it may have been only days, but it was long enough for us to be told to don our outdoor clothes and head for the school playground. It was one carpet of snow and we all set about building not snowmen but a Saxon village.

Please do not imagine we built huge dwelling places, not so. All the buildings clustered together were only a few inches high. But on the scale of things that was probably just as it should have been. We marked out our three fields, one for grain, a second for whatever and the third fallow, i.e. resting without a crop, in a state of preparation for its next crop.

I only remember doing this on one occasion, so I suppose there was a thaw and that was the end of the Saxon village. But it was good fun and the details of that period were reinforced by such ingenuity on the part of the history mistress.

During this first year we began to study Greek mythology. I really enjoyed this subject. The reader may remember that I had discovered this enthralling subject not long before, when perusing the three encyclopaedias which my father had obtained. I have always believed that it is rather neglected in school. It is taught but not enough time is given to the study of it. If more were made of it in the curriculum, I am certain it would become more popular. The stories cannot fail to excite.

Alongside Greek mythology we were also introduced to Shakespeare. *A Midsummer Night's Dream* was the first play which we studied. Always a good choice when introducing children to the Bard.

Interaction in the staff-room is obvious to me now, for not only were we studying this lovely play containing all the most glorious characters, Bottom, Puck, the fairies and a host of others, but the school as a whole was going to put on a big production at the very beginning of the next school year.

The older pupils were playing the main characters, but four of us first years were to play the fairies, namely Peaseblossom, Cobweb, Mustardseed and Moth. I think the four who were chosen were given the roles because we were small. I was to be Peaseblossom.

The play was to be performed on the school lawn, which as I have already described had a rose bed in each corner. It was behind one of the rose beds that we four fairies were to crouch, waiting for the moment when we would spring into action and dance.

We thought we were very important to be included in this senior production and we prepared for our roles by practising day after day during the lunch-break. We would meet the music mistress in the gymnasium, where there was a piano, and to the music of Schubert's *Rosamund* ballet we would rehearse our dance routine. I did not know the name of that beautiful piece of music until years later when I bought a book of music called *Gems of Schubert* and I came upon it again.

After that wonderful experience at eleven years of age I always had a strong desire during my years at school to play the part of Puck. I enjoyed gymnastics, I enjoyed dancing and I loved acting, but sadly the opportunity never arose.

That first year at school had been a very eventful year coinciding as it did with the Blitz. I now realise that I was not unusual in sometimes being worried about something new which I was encountering at school. Children will often toss and turn in their sleep when something is worrying them. They will talk in their sleep too. This it seems I did, to everyone's consternation in the limited space of the air-raid shelter. I was reciting one to ten in German – I never was very proficient at foreign languages and was obviously worried at the time.

Another disrupted night which I recall at that time was when the air raids were not happening every night and we had begun to sleep once again in the house, unless there was a raid in progress.

My father was not sleeping in the house this particular night, it was his turn for duty as fire-watcher at his place of work. Very necessary at that establishment, which contained very little other than paper and cardboard, added to which incendiary bombing was then the order of the day.

My brother, who was five or six years old at the time, awoke during the night. Actually because his eyes were open my mother and I thought he was awake, but he was delirious. He was pointing up to the corner of the ceiling and screaming. Nothing would pacify him and I was instructed by my mother to run and fetch my aunt, who was living two houses from us, so that she might take care of my brother and me while Mum ran across the road to bring back my father.

The next morning my brother said that he remembered a face coming towards him from the corner of the ceiling. I found it very frightening and remember being amazed when, after a visit to the doctor the next day, my mother explained to me that it was caused by my brother having a temperature. I recall that it occurred a few more times when he was unwell, but never again so severely.

Another example of then and now. Then if one talked of having a temperature it was taken to mean that one was hot and lacking energy, but it was never confirmed because it was not usual for a household to be in possession of a thermometer, as it is today.

Normally when one has a very bad dream it is remembered on awakening but is very often so soon forgotten that even on the same day it is difficult if not impossible to recall. It must be a really terrifying dream to remain with someone for the rest of their life. My brother's dream or nightmare was just such an experience which he still remembers.

I had two terrifying dreams when a child, for they were only dreams, I was not unwell at the time, no raging temperature, but they are as clear today as they were at the time they happened.

In the first dream I was sitting in an armchair next to the fire and facing the dining-room table, which was against the opposite wall. On this table lay the body of an aunt. As I watched, her body still remained in its position on the table but at the same time, although still lying there, she began very slowly to sit up. I will not call what I saw a ghost because there was nothing nebulous about it. My aunt was lying there with her arms straight at her sides, and the figure which slowly was rising to a sitting position still had its arms at its side – it was just another figure of my aunt.

I cannot imagine why I dreamed this ghastly dream; my aunt was only a young woman at the time and I was very

147

fond of her, she was not an old lady which could have put the idea of death into the mind of a child. But I was always a little uneasy at the thought of her dying, wondering whether I might have a nightmare on hearing of her death. But when the sad event did occur I had no dream.

The second dream which I have never forgotten occurred when I was about twelve years old. The dreams we have often relate in some way to something which has happened recently, quite often that day, but I cannot imagine what brought about the dream of my aunt – or my second dream, unless my mother had reprimanded me for leaving my gloves lying around.

It was a very short dream. I was walking down the stairs when I saw a glove. I bent down and picked it up, to discover to my horror that it contained a hand.

That was all, but to this day I have never gone to bed knowing there is a pair of gloves visible or lying anywhere that I might see them. During the day, no problem. At night a very different story, of which my husband is aware.

Soon after the Second World War began, food was rationed. To supplement the shortages, my father obtained an allotment and started keeping chickens in our garden. The allotment was about a half a mile away and was another excuse for me to accompany my father in the evenings.

The family in one of the houses which backed on to the allotments allowed my father to keep his gardening equipment in the shed at the end of their garden. The allotment holders held regular competitions, which were good fun, and the produce grown was welcomed by all our relatives. Dad continued to make good use of the allotment for some years after the war and I continued to assist him – if I remember correctly, principally when the strawberries were ripe and at their best.

The chickens were a great hit. Not only did we have a plentiful supply of eggs, but we had the occasional chicken too. This at a time when chicken was a luxury, which now is difficult to imagine. Dad began with three Rhode Island Red hens and they were named after my brother, my cousin who had been bombed out and was still living with us, and me. Their living accommodation was five-star. It was built at the end of the garden, contained on three sides by the back wall, the side fence and the brick wall of the garden shed. The front was completely wire mesh with a door. There was a nesting box on each side and the top half of the rear was their roost, with doors to pull down and fix if my father thought it necessary.

There were two hooks in the ceiling of the cage, from which we would suspend vegetable greenery at a certain height so that the chickens had to flutter up to obtain it. My father said they needed the exercise although they were often quite loose to roam in the garden and they had the normal earth as the base of their run. Seed was always scattered on this to enable them to scratch away at it. They had mash daily, which consisted of I know not what, but I know it was mixed with the cooked peelings of the potatoes.

It seems to be a popular belief in some circles at the moment that children from the cities know very little about what goes on outside their urban lives. How can they possibly be unaware of the lives which other people live when they are deluged by the media continually? Even if viewing television at home does not include watching documentaries or the more enlightening of programmes, surely their time at school must include learning about rural life from a very young age.

I recently heard on the radio that some city children were unaware of where milk came from and in fact they had never heard of a cow. I find these two facts difficult to believe. If, however, they are true, then there exist teachers who are incompetent. In my day as a child we had no visual aids such as television but I am certain we all knew what a cow was and what it produced.

The same can be said for chickens. We must have been very well informed, for I am sure every child was cognisant of the connection between chickens and eggs.

I certainly was, with the newly installed egg producers in our garden. Names spring to mind like Rhode Island Red, Light Sussex, White Leghorn, Minorca and Buff Orpington. There are groups of names which one never forgets; these breeds of chickens were one and another was the many varieties of potatoes which my father grew.

The most exciting event which keeping chickens produced was when a hen went broody. She would sit on the eggs for twenty-one days, at which time we would eagerly await the breaking of eggshells and the emergence of the gorgeous little balls of fluff. There can be few prettier sights than this. It was lovely to see the hen sitting with the tiny chicks peeping out from under her. However, if an egg failed to produce a chick my father would recommend we each held our nose as he cracked the egg to ascertain exactly what was going on inside before rushing off to dispose of the highly pungent egg.

For some weeks following this event I would be despatched regularly to purchase special food for the chicks. Made up of minute ingredients, it was called number one mixture, followed by numbers two and three, which gradually increased in size, by which time I suppose the chicks were able to cope with the normal chicken diet. If only my father were still around he would be able to add so much more interesting information.

If we were unlucky and no hen went broody, which happened occasionally, my father would set off on Sunday morning to buy a dozen day-old chicks. I once asked if they were only a day old, wondering how they could travel without food, and my father told me that they do not eat for a day or two when first hatched.

We would eagerly await his return from the market, quite a long bus journey, carrying his purchase. He had their new home ready for them. It consisted of a large wooden tray about eight inches high covered with large mesh. At one end was an electric light bulb inside a small box made of wire mesh. The tiny chicks would huddle close to this for warmth. If one did not appear to be doing too well it was put in a small box in the gas oven. The oven was lit on the lowest heat and with the door left open we would sit keeping watch. I do not believe we had many that failed to survive. They really were extremely well cared for.

When keeping chickens as a food supplement was no longer necessary. Dad disposed of the chicken coop and built an aviary. He had some quite exotic small birds. That was his new hobby and he derived great enjoyment from it, always making sure the birds were warm in the winter – he was a very caring man. He was always very interested in flora and fauna. Mum would often comment that if they went for a drive it would more often than not be to Epping Forest, where she would remain in the car reading or taking a nap and he would stroll about always 'looking', as she put it. She would exaggerate, saying, 'He can stand looking at a tree for hours.'

As I wrote earlier on, the first three laying hens with which my father began chicken-keeping were named after my brother, my cousin and me. My cousin is one year my junior and during my first year at secondary school she too was entered for a Junior County Scholarship. They were still living with us, and when the letter arrived announcing the results of her examination I was aware of what the envelope contained and stood at the front door, eagerly awaiting their

151

return. When they came into view I ran to meet them and deliver the letter.

She had been awarded the scholarship and during the next four years three more of my cousins were similarly fortunate. After this time the remainder sat the 'Eleven Plus'.

By the summer everything was beginning to settle down again. Air raids were infrequent, my cousin and her parents had been found accommodation and supplied with the bare necessities in the way of furniture and household goods and I had settled in really well at school.

In the meantime Auntie Nellie, of whom I wrote a great deal earlier on, had moved to Devon. Her husband had been called up and was in the army. He was stationed in Devon and Auntie Nellie had decided to find lodgings in Exeter so that she might be near to him. She lodged with a very nice lady who had another spare room and it was suggested that my cousin who was to join me at school after the summer holidays might accompany me to stay with Auntie Nellie for a two-week holiday.

In retrospect I can only presume that in my case the spirit was always willing but the flesh was always weak. My cousin and I were taken to the London station and there put aboard the train, eager to see our aunt as we always were. The guard was informed of our presence and agreed to 'keep an eye' on us. When one considers this was 1941, we were two very young girls and we were alone on a journey from London to Devon, it really was quite an adventure.

We were met by our aunt and taken to her lodgings, where we were made very welcome. I was particularly pleased because the lady of the house allowed me to play her piano and she possessed sheet music which contained tonic sol-fa. We settled in very well, both always happy when we were with Auntie Nellie and her husband.

They took us out and about on trips. I remember watching our uncle catching eels in a river one day. Another day we went to the seaside and I recall seeing rolls of barbed wire on the beach, which I suppose was part of our defence system in the summer of 1941.

But it will come as no surprise to the reader to learn that after a few days I began my plaintive cry of 'I want to go home.' It could only have taken a few days for me to come to this decision because no-one concerned had a telephone, and yet a letter must have been sent to my parents and they must have sent a reply making the arrangements for my cousin and me to return to London after one week instead of the two originally arranged.

We were put on a train once again and once again put in the care of the guard.

When we reached London my mother was waiting for us and, as usual, I was overjoyed at seeing her. I remember being that time a little apprehensive about my reception and not without just cause. After all was said and done, if I could not be happy on holiday with Auntie Nellie, would there ever be hope for me or was I a lost cause?

As we walked along the platform my mother began to reprimand me well and truly. I believed even her patience was beginning to run out, and this time even I was subdued. But then she said something like, 'Wait until your father sees you, he is going to have something to say to you,' and I knew then that I was home and dry. My father would be only too pleased to see me back safe and sound and because he was never the enforcer of discipline in the family, I knew I had by then received from my mother the worst of the scolding that my latest wimpishness was to produce.

9

Will I Want to Go Home?

During the Blitz my church had been slightly damaged. I am not really sure to what extent, but it was enough to decrease the number of church activities if not all of them for some time.

For the remainder of that first year at school I was unable to attend Sunday school and, coupled with the discontinuance of having Sunday lunch with my grandparents, also due to the Blitz, Sundays were not terribly exciting – until by a very fortunate casual meeting between a lady and my mother, I met the girl who was to become my friend for life.

With so many men serving in the armed forces during the war, women were compelled to make up the shortfall in the workforce by going out to work whether they wanted to or not. But if they had children of school-age or under, this ruling did not apply. As both my brother and I were at school, my mother was exempt from this obligation.

However, she did decide to supplement the family income by doing what was called 'out-door work' for the firm which employed my father and had employed her until I was expected. The work which she did for many years was known as 'burrs'. Flat thin cardboard shapes with windows came to my mother in packs of a hundred. My mother had to stick a transparent backing over the window before gluing the two edges together to make a small packet. The

154

transparent inch-square pieces of backing were in little packs of one hundred, and I would earn my pennies by laying them out singly to make the fiddly job of picking them up easier for my mother. She enjoyed her little job, there was no mess involved. I believe the completed packets eventually contained burrs (small drills) used by dentists, but the huge numbers involved remain a mystery to me.

Every Friday my mother would visit her place of employment, which was only a couple of hundred yards away, to collect the wages earned by her labours during the week. One day while waiting she began chatting to another lady who was also an 'out-door worker', only to find that she had a daughter who had recently joined the school which I was attending. In point of fact the school which was so kindly housing all the other schools was her actual school. For sixty years I have wondered why she chose that school when my school was nearer to her home. I will have to ask her – better late than never. However, she was at least able to avail herself of public transport, living close to a bus route which was of no use to me.

During their ensuing conversation my mother must have mentioned that owing to the recent damage which had been inflicted on my church I was no longer attending Sunday school. The lady's daughter was going regularly to the local Congregational Church and it was suggested that I join her.

We became the closest of friends. We were always together, other than at school. Two years later we were not at the same school; my school having returned from evacuation, we were able to return to our own premises.

The Congregational Church, known locally as the Round Chapel, which is self-explanatory, was a large building which also housed a large hall and many other rooms both large and small. We would often liken it to a rabbit warren.

We both became Girl Guides and spent a considerable amount of time at the church. The Guides occupied us a

155

great deal, for as well as the usual weekly meetings we would all meet to discuss and take part in the activities involved in acquiring our various badges.

The church was very active, like my original church, because no church could have been more alive than my church had been, but the services were different. They were more informal than those which I had been used to. Whether the minister was also the Scout master I do not know, but I certainly can remember him taking Sunday morning service attired in his Scout uniform.

Sunday school was not just a Sunday afternoon meeting, we would also meet in the evenings during the week. We were not old enough to encroach on the activities of the older church members, but we were aware that badminton was regularly played and the hall also had some gymnastic apparatus.

The gentleman who was in charge of the Sunday school lived a short distance away in Woodford. He and his wife regularly made us welcome in their home, and if the weather permitted it we would play croquet in their garden.

Once a year the church would hold an event comprising many different competitions. It went on all day Saturday and we would enter for various contests.

One day I entered the sausage-roll and the singing sections. It was all good fun, but girls can be cruel. I remember how we girls all got an attack of the giggles when a young lad stood on the stage singing nicely but going horribly off key, obviously due to his voice breaking at that time.

There seems to be less demand for organisations such as those to which my friend and I belonged. Our 'Girls Club', homework and the church activities took up so much of our leisure time that we were never bored. The television is always cited as the cause of the demise of such organisations, but I think that is too simple an answer. Were there ever many venues for young persons?

There always were churches which encouraged activities for the young and there always were those which did not. It is the same today. And it has to be admitted that it is only the minority of young people who are the least bit interested in going to a church service or attending any church activities. But was it so different years ago?

When I consider the numbers that made up the community in my youth, I realise that the proportion that went to church or met at a club such as ours, was very small. Then, when school or work was over for the day, most people returned to their homes, had a meal and either visited the cinema or remained in for the evening. They would sometimes visit friends. Either way, it would result in sitting chatting together. The only way I can see that television has influenced the evening social activities is by superseding the informal conversations that once took place.

However, although I do not believe the popularity of television, videos etc. can be blamed for the closure of great numbers of organisations, it must be accepted that some associations, such as Guide and Scout groups, are rather depleted. But this it seems is more often because no leaders can be found to run things rather than not enough youngsters being willing to participate.

The one certain detrimental effect television has had is the result of it being a substitute for conversation between children, particularly very young children, and their parents, and family activities. This I consider to be very serious and a subject rather neglected.

Having been for so many years the first teacher to have charge of children experiencing school for the first time, I have always found it obvious from day one which youngsters have been used to conversing and which have spent most of their time at home watching television or videos.

I remember when I was teaching, a particularly horrific

157

well-known film was shown on television one evening. It did not end until 10.30 p.m. and the following day for his 'news' a child told the class about the film. Others had seen it and I kept a record of those children, ready to produce on open evening if the parents of any one of those particular children had queried their child's school progress in any way.

But it doesn't seem fair to blame the advent of television for this situation, the parents who rely solely on this means of keeping their child occupied would have probably counted on the child entertaining himself in any case.

Television produces some superb programmes, but it also produces quite a quantity of unnecessarily silly material, a lot of which is on the children's programmes. If only all children could be encouraged to watch the best of television, they would learn so much in what is a more attractive way than their predecessors had recourse to. Visiting museums and places of interest, and reading, were once the main sources of information.

I seem to have strayed from the subject of the church which my friend and I joined, but the points which have come to mind have reinforced my belief that there never were that many more organisations to which young people could belong. If you are the type of person who likes and seeks the company of others, you will go out and find it.

Maybe my new-found friends at school were an influence or maybe the school environment encouraged all of us, but it is certainly the case that I was aware that life was good, it was interesting and I was enjoying it.

I also at this time joined a small group of children who would meet at the home of an elderly lady who was a music teacher. She would teach us songs to sing, and presumably when we were proficient we were let loose on the unsuspecting public to entertain them. I believe the performances came under the heading of 'Holidays at Home'. In war-time people's holidays were practically non-existent, so I suppose someone had the bright idea of entertaining people to brighten up Saturday evenings. The venture did not last very long. Or perhaps it would be more accurate to say that my participation in it was short. I am not sure which is correct. I remember giving only two performances, one outside the town hall and one in a hall. That was called entertainment; how unsophisticated we were.

About this time I also started to have piano lessons. It was rather a sad occasion, saying goodbye to tonic sol-fa for ever, but I enjoyed my lessons, which took place to the accompaniment of the sound of crunching celery. The music teacher was a very tiny and it seemed at the time a very old Miss Wisdom. During every single music lesson, which obviously coincided with her afternoon tea, she would sit beside me with a plate on which were crackers, a small piece of cheese and sticks of celery. She would vigorously munch her way through this repast while I practised my music. She always reminded me of a little bird pecking away.

I got on quite well with my music, but she and I parted company when she told my mother that I was too fond of making up 'bits of my own'. I never really understood what I did wrong, perhaps I embellished the music with a note here and there.

I had, however, learned enough by the time I left to buy my own choice of music and understand it sufficiently to enable me to play it. It was to be another two years before I began to take lessons again.

We engaged in a great deal of acting at school, and not only in English lessons. The German mistress had always taught us the German versions of well-known songs, one being the

159

hymn 'Holy Night, Silent Night', which I always thought very beautiful when sung in German, although in general it is not my opinion that the German language lends itself to the singing of songs; it is rather guttural, not sweet enough.

In retrospect I think the German mistress was rather optimistic when she suggested we put on a play in German. We were only twelve and thirteen years of age. I cannot remember how much dialogue was contained in the play but we did our best. Whether our accents were intelligible is anyone's guess, but as the play was so well known the dialogue was hardly necessary and I doubt many of the parents would have understood what we were saying had our pronunciation been perfect.

The play was *Snow White and the Seven Dwarfs* and it must have been a farce of the first order. One would imagine that the tallest girl might be chosen to play the part of Snow White and the smallest in the form to take on the roles of the dwarfs. Not in our production. I, the smallest, was to be Snow White, resulting in all the dwarfs being taller and bigger than I. Recently I visited a friend who reminded me that she had been one of the dwarfs and she was always quite tall. But with only the pupils in one form from whom to select the cast, we were rather restricted.

The German mistress and the head girl got together and translated a few of the songs from the original film. They did not exactly translate the songs, they made up appropriate words to the tunes. To this day I remember the words of two songs. The first I as Snow White sang. It went thus:

> *Mein Prinz kommt auf einmal.*
> *Den finde ich auf einmal.*
> *Auf dem schneeweissen Pferd*
> *Kommt er bald.*
> *Und wie glücklich wenn ich*
> *Ihn mir halte.*

160

The other song which I remember was sung by the dwarfs, and when my friend and I met up again recently she reminded me that she had been one of the little men. We sang in unison:

Hi Ho, Hi Ho. Wir kommen
jetzt nach Hause.
Wir arbeiten den ganzen Tag.
Hi Ho, Hi Ho.

We felt quite nostalgic, but I am not sure what our husbands made of it.

A very interesting event took place at this time. At the commencement of one of our German lessons the mistress was accompanied by a very elderly gentleman. He was not very tall, he was Jewish and he sported a quite long white beard. He had spent time in a concentration camp. We must have been aware of his impending visit because I and others had our autograph books ready for him to sign and date. That is the reason for my knowing the exact time when we were rehearsing our production of *Snow White and the Seven Dwarfs*. The poor gentleman had to sit through a performance of the play during the lesson.

It is things like our little play and that visit which helped make our school days so memorable.

We seemed to spend a great deal of time in the Green Room, which was situated under the stage. We were always rehearsing for something and we also liked ferreting around and trying on costumes. Twice there was an 'accident' with the foam fire extinguisher. I never saw the result of it 'accidentally' being set into action but I believe it made quite a mess.

On the whole we were well behaved at school and rules

161

were rigidly enforced. This was accepted as the norm, we had been accustomed to this from birth. We were used to routine not, as I have already chronicled, like many children of today who are fed on demand from birth and go on to expect everything on demand.

So encountering rules and regulations at secondary school would not have been a shock for us; we had been used to them at primary school. The one deterrent worthy of attention was the threat of expulsion, not that I can remember it ever hanging over our heads like the Sword of Damocles. We only ever knew of one girl being expelled, and that was for stealing something belonging to another pupil.

Prefects were our problem. They were always so efficient and they always seemed to be paranoid about hats, winter hats or summer panamas. Hats seemed to be their obsession. What could be easier than enforcing the 'hats must be worn' rule and thereby exerting their authority.

As if the wearing of a panama hat during the summer did not draw enough attention to us, we also had to wear short white socks. The idea of long white socks had not been thought of, not that they would have been a great improvement.

But we were so used to our uniform and we were so very proud of our school that I can only recall it ever being a problem on one occasion. This occurred during the week following a weekend when I had been to a dance on the Saturday, met a young man and visited the cinema with him on the Sunday. Suddenly on the way home from school the following week, attired in panama hat and white socks, I saw him walking toward me. I panicked, turned left and had to make a very long detour home.

It is easy to understand the shocked reaction when the fire extinguisher was set off in the Green Room. But the interest in the Green Room continued, and so did the acting.

I had been given the opportunity to play a small part in

162

the school's *A Midsummer Night's Dream* production and then the main role of Snow White, but my characters were not always so attractive. The next play we performed was *Cinderella*. I was cast as one of the Ugly Sisters. This time I was definitely chosen because I was small, and the other Ugly Sister, who was a very good friend of mine at that time, was chosen, I know she would not be offended by my saying, because she was rather rotund. We had to make great play of hugging each other and sobbing hysterically. We were very enthusiastic, falling about in absolute fits of laughter because I found it difficult to hold on to her.

I wish I had talked at greater length to my parents about my school work. They took a great interest in everything to which they were invited, but I often had the impression that, to my mother, school should have been the thorough learning of the three Rs and more practical subjects, such as domestic science. Not so my father. But he had encouraged me when I was younger and then I believe was content to let the school take over. To see us continually acting, they must have pondered on what we did all day. It is not surprising that my mother so often referred to it as 'that school'.

When I was considering my future career before leaving school, my mother commented that the only useful thing 'that school' had taught me was how to talk my way into anything and how to talk my way out of it again. A profound thought on her part?

At sixteen years of age, the age now for taking the GCSE examinations, we sat the School Certificate. But we took fewer subjects then than appears to be the norm now for the more academically minded pupils. There were obviously many subjects which were compulsory and others where specific choices had to be made.

163

The first subject I 'dropped' was domestic science. Not because it held no interest for me, but because I decided it was something which I could quite happily perform at home.

That, however, is being too flippant, because there were actually two reasons for my making the decision. The first was related to sewing. My mother had always possessed a sewing machine, bought when she married. It was a treadle model and I had been using the machine for some years. I had never made anything significant in the way of clothes, but I had, under instruction from Mum, made items such as hankies and very simple aprons. But the point was that I was proficient in the use of the treadle sewing machine and was annoyed when the domestic science mistress continually told me to slow down.

There are certain attributes and traits both mental and physical which we inherit and over which we have no control. One of these in my family is doing everything at a rate of knots. My mother at eighty-five years of age was still running up the stairs, and believe me I really mean running, in her eagerness to show us something. My sister-in-law reminded me of this only recently. I and my daughters also have the tendency to do everything at speed, and my reprimand from the domestic science mistress was brought to my mind when I watched my elder daughter at a very young age using my treadle sewing machine. I called my husband to watch the phenomenal sight of her little legs going at breakneck speed. We laughed hysterically, while she failed to see the funny side of it.

The other part of the domestic science subject was cookery. To this day I do not appreciate food which has been messed about with, titivated or prettied up, call it what you will. I like my food to be fairly plain but certainly hot and tasty. Someone once told me that my taste buds hadn't matured. If that means I prefer my meals freshly cooked and hot instead of luke warm and pretty, then so be it.

164

This brings me to the second reason for giving up the subject. We were told we were going to make a rhubarb pie. As I have just written, I like my meals to be tasty. If I have a pie, be its filling meat or fruit, I look forward to eating the filling with the added enjoyment of the pastry. But the pastry is only an addition to the meat or fruit, one could have a nice meal without the pastry, whereas one would not be satisfied with the pastry minus the meat or fruit.

Therefore when we came to make the rhubarb pie I would have been satisfied with cooking the rhubarb, making the pastry, covering the former with the latter and popping it in the oven.

Oh, no. I suppose we cooked the rhubarb first, but it really isn't important, because what is forever imprinted on my mind is the time spent on the pastry.

We made it, we lined the dish with it and then proceeded to 'play' with it. First we covered the fruit, then we made rose petals, rose buds and rose leaves. We placed them artistically all over the pies and then popped them into the ovens.

By the time we had a base, a top and roses all made of pastry, the filling was the least important ingredient in the pie. I could not give up domestic science fast enough.

About this time Auntie Nellie returned from Exeter because her husband had been posted closer to home, and she settled in a flat within walking distance of my home.

Soon I was informed by my mother that both Auntie Nellie and her sister were pregnant. Both their husbands were in the army, and the other aunt already had a three-year-old son.

Pregnancies were not something much discussed in the presence of a twelve-year-old in those days unless something unusual warranted it. Therefore I knew very little about their progress until Auntie Nellie fell down the town hall steps. She was quite far advanced in her pregnancy by that time, and an ambulance was called to whisk her off to hospital.

It must not be forgotten that this was at the time when scans were unheard of and even X-rays in pregnancies were not a routine procedure. But an X-ray was taken and the doctor confronted Auntie Nellie with the news that she should go home and prepare for two babies.

At least she had a few weeks to put the change of plans into operation. Five years previously her sister had had no idea that she was to be the mother of twins until they actually arrived.

It was a hectic time and I helped my aunt prepare for the double event. I accompanied her when she purchased a second cot and ordered a twin pram, a well-known make, with a hood at each end.

It never occurred to me at the time but my other aunt probably felt a little neglected. Her second son was born six weeks before Auntie Nellie's twins, and she also had her small boy to care for. I do know my mother, other aunts and grandmother were all very supportive, but it does seem as if the attention was focused on the aunt expecting the twins.

The time arrived for the expected birth of the twins and my aunt went into labour and was duly taken to the hospital. It was a false alarm, but as the babies were due anyway, it was decided she should remain in hospital until they were born.

I had spent a great deal of time with her in the weeks leading up to her admission and was eager to visit her, but hospital visiting then and for many years after was very strictly controlled: only half an hour each evening and half an hour on Sundays and one afternoon during the week,

166

and no more than two visitors were allowed at one time for each patient. Visitors would wait patiently outside the doors to the wards during the allotted half-hour for their turn to take their place at the patient's bedside. And on no account would anyone under fourteen years of age be allowed to visit a patient. I can only suppose it was the school-leaving age which dictated that ruling.

Now visiting is more lax and allowed on and off during every day. Not only are visitors continually going in and out of the hospitals but patients stroll in and out, standing outside the entrance so that they might indulge in their pastime of smoking. I and many other persons of my generation find it absolutely incomprehensible that patients are allowed to stroll up and down a hospital drive, which is a public thoroughfare, dressed in their nighties, pyjamas, dressing gowns and fluffy slippers or trainers. Added to which it is not unusual to witness a patient strolling along still attached to a mobile drip.

This lax attitude hardly seems designed to prevent the introduction of germs into the hospital environment.

However, the change in visiting rules and regulations is even more evident in the maternity wards. When my children were born, only husbands were allowed to visit and then only for half an hour in the evening, apart from the easing of this restriction for half an hour on Sunday afternoons when the two grandmothers were permitted to visit the new mums, but not the babies – they were only brought from the nursery to be fed.

I am certain the nursing staff would find their workload easier and the patients would benefit if visitors were not strolling around the wards all day.

The siblings of new babies are permitted to visit the mum and new baby. It comes under the heading of that popular word 'bonding'. I cannot say that I had any problems bonding with my brother when he arrived. It is true I was

five years old by then and therefore old enough to understand the situation more clearly than might be the case with
younger siblings, but one might also say that having been
the only child for five years, it would have been understandable if I had felt neglected on the arrival of a baby, but it
was not so.

The only other personal experience I have was the arrival
of number two daughter when number one daughter was
only twenty-two months old. There was no problem with
bonding on that occasion either.

In neither of these examples was the sibling allowed to
visit mum and baby during their stay in hospital.

But I have strayed from the story of Auntie Nellie waiting
patiently for her twins to arrive.

I cannot think why I should have arrived at the hospital
clutching a bundle of comics. Perhaps that was the only
personal gift that I could think of. But I made my way to
the door of the large ward and there met my grandmother.

I was trying desperately to keep a low profile but, as I
was only just thirteen and small for my age, it wasn't long
before the sister spotted me. She approached us in that very
authoritative manner which ward sisters thankfully have
and informed my grandmother that I was too young to be
allowed to enter the ward. Whereupon my grandmother put
me in one of the most embarrassing of situations, probably
the most at that time, by telling the sister that I was small
for my age but that I must have been old enough because I
was a Girl Guide. How I cringed. Young girls are easily
embarrassed, often by their mothers, and by their grandmothers too, it seems. Only the most stalwart of young girls
would not have cringed over such a remark. Either the
sister was completely nonplussed by Big Nan's comment,
which seems unlikely – sisters are not easily surprised and
confused – or she saw the funny side of it and may have felt

168

sorry for me. Whatever the reason, she very kindly let me enter with my comics to visit Auntie Nellie.

The twins, a boy and a girl, were born in different months. One arriving at 11.45 p.m. on July 31st and the other at 12.45 a.m. on August 1st, both weighing over five pounds.

They were beautiful babies and, as was to be expected, I was there ready and eager to help on her return from hospital – school holiday time. My uncle was given compassionate leave by the army and I accompanied him when he went to collect his wife and babies and take them home. But my mother would not allow me to visit again until my uncle had returned to barracks.

Those first few months must have been very difficult for my aunt: two new babies, no husband to assist, no disposable nappies, no washing machine, no tumble-dryer, not even a spin-dryer, no freezer, not even a refrigerator to keep food fresh from one day to the next. But she did have relatives and friends. A little respite during the day for a quiet cup of tea with a friend can make a great difference when you are 'on duty' alone every twenty-four hours.

I would often call in on my way home from school and every Saturday I would visit from early in the morning and remain all day. I helped bath the twins, dress them and feed the baby whose turn it was to be bottle-fed. Then I would push them in their twin pram, visiting my friend during my walk. People would continually stop to admire them. They looked so beautiful, twins were then a more uncommon sight than today. A midwife recently told me that IVF treatment often results in the birth of twins and even triplets.

But when the babies were about four months old their mother had to go into hospital. As a thirteen-year-old I was curious as to the reason for this but did not ask my mother for an explanation, probably aware that she would not have

169

been very forthcoming, but I did hear the word afterbirth mentioned and wondered what it was.

My uncle was again allowed compassionate leave and for one week he cared for the babies fantastically with the assistance of relatives, but unfortunately he had to return to duty, and although my mother and my aunt each offered to care for a baby, it was decided by my uncle that they should not be separated and so they went to stay in a council-run establishment for about a week.

Auntie Nellie returned from hospital and went with my grandmother to fetch her babies home. My grandmother always insisted the babies were not really fit at that time. It is history now. Within a few days it was discovered that the babies had gastro-enteritis. I realised that the situation was serious when my grandmother visited us and spoke to my mother in that confidential manner which adults always took on when we were young if they didn't think we should hear the details.

I was very upset, particularly when I was told that I was not to visit my aunt and the twins. I had spent so much time in my aunt's company before her return to hospital that it was inevitable that I should want to help her with the babies at this difficult time. But my mother's word was final and I was never to see the twins again.

I am told that it was more common for gastro-enteritis to prove fatal for babies at that time than now. Our understanding of the necessity for cleanliness and all-round hygiene, including conditions and practices which are conducive to maintaining health and preventing disease, has certainly helped, together with the huge amount of progress which has been made in medical care, and gastro-enteritis is not the problem it appears to have once been.

Most people's living conditions have so improved over the intervening years since the end of the Second World

War that it is not difficult to see that this alone contributed in large measure to helping solve the problem of hygiene.

Auntie Nellie's baby girl died in December. The little boy lingered for longer and eventually died in hospital about six weeks later. Everyone in the family was heart-broken. Auntie Nellie was and still is the loveliest aunt in the world. She adored all of us, and her own babies had been so beautiful, but she had lost them both.

Because her husband was in the army she was living alone, but fortunately she was part of our extended family and that must have helped her to cope. But it must have been heart-breaking for her to see her sister, who lived in the same road, with the baby who was born six weeks before the twins. But it never was and still is not in her nature to be bitter. She would visit her sister and make a fuss of her baby. This I know for fact because I was often there with them.

About the time when the twins died, the other aunt's husband was sent abroad, leaving her with the new baby and a four-year-old. This was not unusual at the time; hundreds of families were in the same situation, but this family had been completely 'bombed out', as it was referred to then. Not a stick remained of their beautiful home. They had eventually found a flat and the authorities had supplied them with the bare essentials in the way of furniture and household effects – just enough to make the flat habitable. Then Uncle was sent to Ceylon, as it was then called, for three and a half years.

I was very fond of my uncle and I wrote to him while he was abroad. He asked me to help my aunt by looking after the baby while she went shopping and also when she went to the hairdresser's. Her husband adored her and always liked to see her well groomed.

I went regularly after school to babysit the two children

171

while she was at the hairdresser's, and on Saturday mornings I would look after the baby while she, accompanied by her other son, would do the shopping for the weekend.

I recall a few times taking the baby into the Anderson shelter when the air-raid siren went and was surprised to find it rather a bare, inhospitable refuge. Not like my shelter at home.

But by then the air raids were not so frequent and most people used them only intermittently, when the occasion arose – until 1944, when the V1s started to arrive and we took to our shelters regularly again.

When I had been at senior school for three years, my own school returned from evacuation. I have already described the difference in the actual school buildings. But although our premises were not modern and sumptuous the building itself was old and impressive, with its Oak Staircase.

We were very happy to return to our own school, which was of high repute. Not all school heads had a PhD. Our Dr Hunt was a lady to be proud of. She ran 'a tight ship', which was probably not appreciated at the time by all the pupils but one realises in later years how advantageous it was to all concerned.

She rarely wore her gown, but when she did we knew as she stood centre stage that she had something important to impart.

On one occasion it was to tell us that the government had issued a statement announcing the commencement of the V1 attacks. These were jet-propelled flying bombs also known by everyone as 'doodlebugs'. That was an important announcement and was recognised as such, I am sure.

The other two occasions I recall seem rather frivolous now but at the time were obviously important to Dr Hunt. The first concerned the wearing of snoods. They were ornamental hairnets, usually crocheted, and had become popular because ladies, who were then a large part of the workforce, particularly in places of war-work, were obliged to wear them to control their hair. And as often happens, the fashion spread out to the population in general. But it wasn't going to become the latest craze in our school. Dr Hunt announced that 'onion bags' were no longer to be worn either at school or on the journey to and from school. 'They did not enhance the school uniform.'

The second issue which she clearly felt strongly about was the arrival now and again of an American serviceman outside the school at home-time in the afternoon.

Teenagers are far more mature and worldly-wise now than we were all those years ago, but nevertheless even then there were girls at the school until they were almost nineteen years of age. It seems quite understandable that the older pupils might have met American servicemen during the weekend.

Obviously Dr Hunt did not see it quite like that and she announced that there would be no more American service-men outside her school.

I am absolutely certain we never saw another American or a snood.

The summer of 1944 saw the commencement of a very busy year for everyone. The invasion of Normandy took place in June, and when we went swimming, on the way back to school we would delay crossing the main road in the hope that an army convoy would suddenly appear and prevent us from crossing for a little time. Stupid girls!

A few days after the invasion saw the first attack by the flying bombs (V1s). I remember the first one we saw going across the sky. It appeared to be a very small aircraft with flames issuing from the rear and it made a strange humming noise, which suddenly stopped, and after gliding along for some seconds it nose-dived. We all thought it was an aeroplane which had crashed, until it was announced the next day that this was Germany's new weapon – the V1.

Back to the shelter. For some eighty days in June, July and August the V1 attacks were heavy, and during that period we slept in the shelter as a matter of course, not waiting for the air-raid warning to sound.

Our relatives had long gone to their new abode, but we were not to be alone in our shelter because the baker who had owned our house, No. 1, which he had sold to my father, also owned No. 3, and he had sold that house to our best friends. The lady of the house had been at school with my mother, and I always called her and her husband Auntie and Uncle. Uncle was in the army, so Auntie and her two sons joined us in the shelter.

Once again we were very comfortable. There were two bunks on each side for my father and the three boys, and mattresses on the floor to accommodate Mum, Auntie and me. I was in the middle. What an unenviable position to be in!

I was continually berated from both sides. It seems not without justification, for in later years when I was in the company of both, they would jokingly join forces and remind me that I was a thorough nuisance in those bygone days by continually sitting up to straighten out all the bed-clothes. First the sheet, then the blankets etc., everything had to be smoothed out and neat.

But I enjoyed those weeks in the shelter at that time simply because it was rather like watching a regular 'soap' on television. When my father had left the shelter to walk around and meet other men to pass the time until bed-time, and the boys were all asleep, my mother and aunt would chat non-stop. I heard all the family and local gossip which normally I would not have been allowed to listen to.

There was one particular item of scandal which my aunt told to my mother which intrigued me to the extent that I looked forward each night to the next instalment of the story. I was just fifteen years of age and, believe it or not, I would not have been privy to this conversation had they realised that I was awake.

Because the flying bombs were like a very small aeroplane, a warning could be given when they were on their way and people had the chance to take shelter if they so wished. We got quite used to seeing them. When their engines stopped and suddenly there was complete silence and they came down, we got to know, according to where they appeared to nose-dive, in which area they would land. It was a very scary feeling, having heard the sinister humming sound, then complete silence, waiting for the explosion.

During this period if there was a terrific explosion fairly close due to a doodlebug, my father and two uncles would be despatched on their bicycles to the home of the aunt with the two little boys, to make sure all was well. They would meet at the house and stay awhile to give moral support before returning to their own homes or shelters.

My father, like many others, took to spotting V1s on his firm's roof. Sometimes the flying bomb would do strange things, like going round in circles or veering in a different direction when the engine stopped. Dad told me on my return from school one day that from his firm's roof he had watched a doodlebug cut out when it was above my school and he was ready to descend hastily and make his way to the school when it turned around and glided for a little way before nose-diving.

In the spring of 1944 our Girl Guide company began preparing to go camping in the summer of that year. We were busy making the preparations for this event and I was as enthusiastic as the other girls. But all the time I won-

175

dered, although it was three years since I had gone to Devon for two weeks but had returned after one week, would I be able to remain for the whole week of camping without wanting to go home? In retrospect I realise that by then I would have been fine, but nevertheless I own that when the flying bomb attacks began in June of that year and our camping trip was cancelled, I heaved a great sigh of relief. I admit now that the question in the back of my mind had always been, 'Will I want to go home?' I think I was 'saved by the bell'.

But at least with the flying bombs we had warning of their approach, whereas for the V2 rocket attacks which began in the early autumn of that year there was no warning. One just heard the explosion.

This last paragraph brings to mind a story from that time.

Sundays were always quiet and peaceful. No shops opened on Sundays other than the local baker's to sell fresh baked bread. Incidentally, every district also had one week-day, usually Wednesday or Thursday, when the shops only opened during the morning. These were known as 'half-day closing days'. This practice was strictly adhered to. Even shops in London's West End participated in the 'half-day closing' routine one day each week. This practice continued for many years. When my own children were babies, it was my usual daily routine to shop during the afternoon when all household chores had been completed. Except for 'half-day closing' day, when anything I wished to purchase would have to be bought before one o'clock.

Sundays, as I have said, were always very quiet, apart from the occasional Salvation Army band. Streets more or less devoid of cars even during the working week saw minimal activity on Sundays. It is difficult for persons of even my generation to recall how silent the streets must have been.

176

Suddenly on this particular Sunday morning there was the most horrendous explosion.

It had to be a V2 rocket, otherwise for every other form of air raid, be it aeroplane or flying bomb, we would have had an air-raid warning.

We all rushed into the street and could see the evidence in the sky. It was black with smoke or dust. It was the closest a rocket came to my home, as the crow flies, it was about three hundred yards away.

My father went running towards it, as did all the local men. We knew it had landed in a very built-up area, but when Dad returned he informed us that it was the consensus of opinion that there had been only one fatal casualty, who they thought might be the watchman in the factory.

How fortunate that the rocket had landed in the road on a Sunday, because the spot where it landed was between the huge clothing factory on one side of the road and a school on the opposite side. Imagine the casualties there could have been had the rocket landed there during a weekday.

The most interesting thing concerning this incident was the story which we heard a few days later. It seems a small boy of four years of age who lived in the area was playing in his garden at the time the rocket fell. He told his parents that he saw a big pointed thing like a pencil come down from the sky as the 'big bang' went. Did he see the rocket? I thought at the time that it was likely and am still of that opinion; it is unlikely a small child could make up a story such as that.

Intermittently these attacks continued until March the following year, when they ceased altogether about six weeks before the war in Europe came to an end.

*

It was during the final year of the war – from June 1944, when the doodlebugs first appeared, until May the following year – that we girls were working and revising for our School Certificate examinations, which we sat in 1945. How we revised with so much going on at that time I shall never understand. It seems to me now that the news alone was enough to impair one's concentration, what with the over-running of Europe, beginning with the famous D-Day landing, the liberating gradually of all the thousands of poor victims who were still lucky enough to be alive in the concentration camps and eventually the ending of the war in Europe (albeit the war in the Far East was continuing), together with flying bombs, rockets and the 'sleeping in the shelter routine' on the home front. I understand that the fighting in Europe did not physically affect us but it was nevertheless a very unsettling time. Sad things were happening and joyous events were taking place. Hopes were high for a better future on the horizon.

My friend and I began to spread our wings a little. I was just fifteen years of age and we were not allowed to go to the cinema during the evening, but a concession was obviously made and we would go on Saturday during the afternoon and return home in the early evening. Going to the cinema in those days was far more popular than it is today. There were no set performances The programmes were continuous, and always included the 'big' film, sometimes a 'B' film, a cartoon, forthcoming attractions and the news. There was no other way to see the news, and without the cinema newsreel we would never have been able to witness events which were happening during the six years of war.

Our grandchildren think it very strange that we more often than not saw the end of the film before the beginning.

But that was how it was. By early evening there were always queues outside the cinema, different queues for various seats, and as people emerged from the cinema others would be allowed in. Sometimes two people going to the cinema together would have to accept separate seats until the end of a film, when it was likely that they might find two seats together.

At least by the time I was fifteen I looked fifteen. Once or twice before then, when my friend and I had gone to the cinema in the afternoon, I had had to keep out of sight of the ticket office, for although I was fourteen years of age, and therefore old enough to see an 'A' certificate film if accompanied by an adult, I did not look old enough, whereas my friend, who was younger than me, had no trouble obtaining the tickets. That really hurt.

So, when we began this late afternoon-early evening routine a whole new programme was set in motion.

We would go to the cinema and on returning it would be to my house we would make our way. By the time we reached home my parents and my brother would have left to visit the cinema, leaving my friend and me with the house to ourselves.

We always prepared the same repast, which we would set out very nicely. It consisted of a tin of pilchards in tomato sauce, a dish of beetroot and a plate of thinly sliced bread and butter – thinly sliced was a necessity. Followed by a cup of tea.

When we had completed the washing-up we would make our way to my friend's home, where we would spend a little time before she and her father would accompany me back to my home. And yes of course, this was immediately followed by their return journey.

I also began to go out more with my mother. I believe the time had probably come when she realised that I should be allowed some choice in what I should wear, and we would make the occasional trip to Oxford Street to buy my clothes.

Do all mothers embarrass their daughters and sons? I have mentioned the faux pas made by Grandmother when she informed the ward sister that I was old enough to enter the hospital ward because I was a Girl Guide, and my mother was also able to cause me embarrassment, but not out of ignorance of the subject. Usually it was because she did not suffer fools gladly or because she was not willing to be fobbed off by a fatuous remark by someone who was trying to sell her something.

We were once shopping for a new dress for me. I was very attracted to one particular dress and the assistant was giving her very best sales talk to me under the mistaken impression that I was buying it. But my mother was paying for the garment. I was never given pocket money, and Saturday jobs or working during school holidays were unheard of. So when the lady commented that a feature of the dress was popular due to its resemblance to the American servicemen's tunics, my mother quickly informed her that I was not an American serviceman.

My friend never had this problem with her mother, a lovely gentle lady who thought that her daughter knew more about the prevailing fashions than she did and therefore gave her the benefit of the doubt. Not so my mother; she was not so easily hoodwinked. The result was usually a compromise until one day the question of a new pair of 'best' shoes reared its ugly head.

Wedge heels had suddenly appeared on the fashion scene and my friend had been allowed – as usual – to buy a pair. I can still see them in my mind's eye. The actual wedge was very, very low, which would have been no use to me. I was not tall enough, I needed a little heel. But they really suited

180

my friend and they were lovely, very smart, green suede with the daintiest of tan decoration.

Oh how I longed for a pair of wedge-heeled shoes. Pleadings and tears were of no avail and I settled for a pair of maroon patent-leather, Cuban-heeled, lace-up shoes. Actually they were rather nice and I have a photograph of my friend and me wearing our new shoes. She too remembers the episode in our young lives.

My mother was rather strict, but this was not unusual at that time. When I compare it to the more liberal approach in many of today's families I firmly believe that we were the more fortunate. We were kept on a tight rein but it was in our own interests and because our parents were concerned for our welfare. My friends and I never rebelled, perhaps at the back of our minds we understood that our parents cared even to the point of being unpopular with us now and again.

But there were two occasions I believe when my mother overdid her position of authority.

The first occurred when I was about sixteen years of age. My friend and I were alone in the house and we decided between us that she would set my hair with hairpins. Nothing terribly dramatic – just twisting hair and keeping it in place. The problem was that I have very wavy hair and Mum absolutely forbade me to pin it or set it in any way, which was completely unreasonable on her part, but that was the rule.

When she arrived home and saw me complete with hair clips (creating for me a new hair-style as I thought) she berated me to such an extent that although it had no effect on me – I was used to being told off and knew that her anger would very quickly subside – it reduced my friend to tears on seeing me so severely reprimanded.

Later in the evening when it was time for my friend to go home, Mum was so concerned that her eyes still showed that she had been crying that she very gently applied a little face-powder around my friend's eyes.

When I was just about sixteen years of age a girl from my school joined our Girls' Club. From that day until now the friendship of two became a threesome. I cannot recollect us ever having an argument. There never were three closer friends. In retrospect it seems we were always just happy to be in the company of each other. We always knew that one of us would have the other two as our bridesmaids, the second to marry would have one as a bridesmaid and the last of the trio would be unable to have either friend to accompany her down the aisle on her wedding day. People who have never experienced such a friendship can never know what they have missed. We were inseparable, and when we all married, with our husbands, we became six very good friends.

It was the new friend who recently reminded me of the second time that my mother overstepped her position of authority.

This friend and I each have two very competent daughters whose careers we were discussing, when my friend suddenly remembered an incident which occurred when I was just eighteen years of age.

I had seen an advertisement in the newspaper for young ladies to train to be officers in the WRENS. This idea rather appealed to me and I sent off for the necessary information. When this arrived my mother did not approve, and to deter me threatened that my 'room' would not be available when I came home on leave. She considered the whole idea a nonsense and promptly threw the information and forms on the fire.

When I later saw my friend she enquired about the

182

information which I had sent for and asked me what my mother had thought of the idea. I told her that Mum had thrown it on the fire. My friend remembered that her own answer on hearing this had been just to say, 'Oh.'

We laughed, both imagining what our own daughters' reactions would have been under similar circumstances.

But had I felt very strongly about the WRENS as a career, I know deep down that all the encouragement required would have been forthcoming from my mother and my father. My mother always had a kind of quick no-nonsense attitude. She never dithered or was indecisive and was always ready to help in a practical and emotional sense. One always felt that she could be depended upon and I could quote so many, many examples of this.

Two instances of her 'off the cuff' retorts which made me a little embarrassed happened when we were shopping.

The first occurred in the grocer's shop. A lady was being served and the grocer was marking her ration books, as was the norm. When the lady had left the shop it was my mother's turn to be served. The grocer, who knew us quite well, asked my mother if she did not think the lady deserved a medal for having twelve children. Whereupon Mum replied, 'No, I think I should have the medal for only having two. Anyone can have twelve children.'

The second occasion was when we approached the greengrocer's shop, which was fronted by a beautiful display of fruit. My mother requested five lemons, pointing to the lemons as she spoke. The assistant put five lemons from the back of the pile into a bag. My mother reminded him that she wanted the ones on display. The gentleman said that they were all the same. To which Mum commented that in that case he would not mind giving her those from the front. She got those she requested. From the top, I might add. She usually got what she wanted because she was always very polite and not unreasonable just quietly determined.

As I have already stated, the final year of the war was a very busy time for my year at school, but this did not prevent our form and the school as a whole from participating in extra-curricular activities.

Our form put on a whole programme of entertainment. The main feature was a play, supported by various other acts, including solo vocalists and very short sketches. It was all extremely good fun and I hope the audience derived as much entertainment and pleasure from it as we did.

Another extra-curricular activity which took place during that year was far more important. This was the school's production of Handel's *Messiah*.

I was very fortunate in being given the chance to participate. We spent a lot of time learning and practising this great work, which was to be performed in the Congregational Church close by – the church which my friend and I attended.

I recall helping to carry chairs from school to the church during the morning of the day of the performance. I can only assume that although there would be ample seating to accommodate the audience, a number of extra chairs would be needed for the choir and so we transported them to the venue.

I went home for lunch that day and during the lunch-break I visited the post office close by. We were friendly with the postmistress and after our business was completed she commented that she was looking forward to attending my school's production of the *Messiah* that day. I was so embarrassed when she spoke of it in the hearing of other customers, it being a newsagent's and tobacconist's as well as a post office, and also at the thought of her going along to watch, that I did not return to school that afternoon and therefore did not attend the performance. I have regretted it ever since, angry with myself for being so stupid. I was so pleased to be in the choir, I adored the music and the singing and was never shy when acting; why I could not face the actual performance is a complete mystery to me.

It would have been nice to bring this chapter to a close on a happy note, but unfortunately at this time the family, who were all so happy that Auntie Nellie was again expecting a baby, were to have a shadow cast over their Christmas. Auntie gave birth to a beautiful little girl on that Christmas Day but sadly the baby died of pneumonia on Boxing Day. She once again accepted that which fate had determined for her. She had no more children but continued to be the loving, favourite aunt of all her nieces and nephews.

10

I Will Never Go Home

I have attempted in previous chapters to describe various episodes when I have wanted to go home, when going home was a necessity, or so it seemed to me and to everyone else who was concerned about me at the time.

All of these occurrences took place when I was a child, and happily the problem resolved itself, due, I am absolutely certain, to the way it was dealt with by my mother and various other adults. There was never a great deal of fuss made on the various occasions and in that way I am sure it was assisted in just fading into the distance – to become an exercise in growing up.

However, I would be lying if I were to say that I have never wished again to go home. But that word 'home' does not mean the house where I was born and lived until I married. It means the area where all my relatives and friends live. It does not now mean the actual borough of London where I was brought up but the area to which each and every one of them has moved.

The only time that I felt a really strong, desperate desire to go home – to be cosseted not only by my husband but by my mother, father, brother and others – was one year after I married, when at the end of a full-term healthy pregnancy something went wrong and our baby was stillborn.

I only document this experience to set forth the difference in procedures then and now.

The stillbirth of our baby happened a long, long time ago. I did not have a Caesarean section but was not fully conscious, and when I floated back for a few minutes to reality, somehow aware that the baby was dead, I asked to see him. The doctor's actual reply was, 'I think best not, don't you?' I never asked again and therefore I never saw him.

Those were the days when one did not question authority and that doctor was 'authority'.

I was in hospital in a single room for nearly three weeks. No television and no-one to talk to. Only husbands were allowed to visit and they were only permitted half an hour each evening. There was one concession to this strict ruling, however: mothers were allowed to visit for half an hour on Sunday afternoons.

I am not sure if anyone was ever aware of my father's visit to me. He somehow managed to talk those in charge into allowing him to visit me, just once. It seems I had a fancy for pineapple and I cannot remember whether he was successful or unsuccessful in satisfying my wish. He could usually be relied upon to somehow obtain the unobtainable, but this was at a time when even common or garden bananas were a rarity. If he produced the pineapple, it would have been given to the nurses, as was the box of fancy pastries which Auntie Nellie deposited at the reception desk.

I truly do not remember requesting to go home at any time during my long stay. Perhaps Dr Hunt's long lecture one day in school on self-discipline was serving a purpose.

No-one made a lot of fuss. What had happened had happened. End of story. The attitude of everyone concerned was so different to that of today, which I attempt to describe later in this chapter.

I desperately wanted to see the baby but never asked again. Perhaps I should have made more fuss. This is difficult when no-one is mentioning a subject. Only my husband and our mothers saw him. Many years later my mother described him to me.

I do not think one is justified in accusing others of making a wrong decision if one is certain that they did it for the best of reasons. In my case, for my own good. Or so they all thought at the time. They were wrong. It took me forty-five years to suddenly set off to find where our baby was buried. But I did find the spot. I was not able to see him but eventually I was able to say goodbye.

Maybe we have taken the policy of a plentiful supply of sympathy and support too far and in that way do not assist the parents in coming to terms with the situation. It has to be faced at some time. The time has to come, as the song says, when one must pick oneself up, dust oneself down and start all over again.

I like to think that I did just that when I came out of hospital, but how I longed to be back home. Yes, 'home', real 'home', surrounded by family and friends. That is what one needs at a time like that, family and friends. Not all the counselling in the world can take their place.

It is often said that life is a compromise, and maybe the answer in such a situation is compromise between the procedure adopted by the hospital staff to me, which was not to refer at any time to what had happened – I was not even visited by my GP when I returned home – and the procedure if it happens today.

A midwife recently informed me that now hospital and staff will go to virtually any lengths to accommodate the wishes of the parents in such a situation. Guidelines to procedure are extremely sympathetic and caring in their purpose. It is recognised that the overwhelming recollection will be the horror of the stillbirth experience and the hushed sounds after the delivery. The helping professional can assist the couple in thinking of ways that they can create memories, not of the shock of the stillbirth but of the baby itself.

It is recognised that if the parents for some reason did not see the baby after the delivery, they may benefit from having this option offered to them again. But they should not be pressured into seeing or holding their baby if they find it too difficult. However, as many options as possible should be offered so that they will have some memory of their baby to assist them in the process of mourning.

Most parents wish to have time alone with their baby. They hold it, are encouraged to unwrap and look at it and are given the opportunity to have a photograph taken of the baby, or they may want a photograph of themselves holding the baby. Every avenue should be explored to respect the parents' wishes. If the parents do not want the photograph, the helping professional may suggest that it be kept in the hospital files in case the couple change their minds at any time. It is a traumatic time and a wrong decision made in haste cannot be rectified.

Practical help includes advice on burial arrangements. Whether to have a service is an important decision to discuss. The parents may want to have a memorial site to visit. The helping professional should ascertain whether the cemetery in which the baby will be buried allows individualised markers or only allows burial in an anonymous plot in its infant section.

The parents should be aware of any choices they can make, which should include what the baby will wear, what special keepsake will be placed with the baby in the casket if they so wish, and any other special involvement by the parents which will give them emotional support in the coming months.

During the first few weeks after the stillbirth the bereaved parents may wish to ask many questions, and an early appointment should be made before the mother is discharged from hospital to give them this opportunity.

It is now emphasised how important is the supportive role of the general practitioner at this time. I certainly would have appreciated it had it been forthcoming.

The hospital doctor had told me to wait two years before becoming pregnant again, owing to the fact that I had had a 'rum do', as he put it, but the doctor at the local clinic suggested I wait only three months. She won. We took her advice and we were soon once again expecting a baby.

We decided to buy a house, but it was 1952 and the housing situation had not recovered since the war. When a couple married they either began married life with relatives or, if they were lucky, occupied a flat which had become vacant in a house which belonged to a friend of a friend of a friend.

Buying a house was not an easy option. Mortgages were far more difficult to obtain than they are now. No hundred per cent mortgages, ninety per cent or even lower were available, and if and when you were offered one, the length of time for repayment was quite short when one considers how young we were. We paid and lost the fees for three building society surveys before realising how difficult it was going to be. The estate agents must have known the situation but gaily went on raising our hopes.

Eventually we lowered our sights, my father loaned us the deposit and we managed to find a property in which the top flat was already let. It was called a part-vacant-possession property and was therefore cheaper than a fully vacant property. Life was beginning to look rosy again.

Within a few months our elder daughter was born and the couple who lived upstairs had moved out. We immediately decided to sell up and move.

I then made the big mistake of agreeing to move even

further away from family and friends when we bought a modern house in north London.

I felt terribly isolated. All the other people living near had bought the houses when they were built in the late 1930s and were of a different generation. Their children, who were of my generation, were married with children of their own and living upstairs in their parents' houses, still in close contact with family and friends. We were outsiders.

But being a full-time housewife then, with no labour-saving devices, daily shopping and two small children to care for, one soon settled into a very contented routine.

The children were not old enough to go to school and playgroups were a thing of the future. Their socialising was conducted when shopping daily and when family or friends visited us. I do not believe they were deprived by not going to a playgroup; a leading sociologist once likened play-groups to open warfare. Having less than two years' differ-ence in their ages enabled them to be always the closest of companions.

After we had been married for six years I began to be rather bored with never seeing or talking to anyone of my own age during the weekdays and I had a good idea – or so we thought at the time.

Every parade of shops had a haberdasher's. We had one in our own parade of shops. They sold wool, sewing materials, small clothing items and baby and children's wear quite often. I thought we could buy such a shop, complete with living accommodation, which I could run while my husband continued to work in the City. I could be at home with the children and also doing something interesting.

We found just the shop we were looking for (just outside London) in Essex. Everything was arranged, we sold our house and then the Chancellor of the Exchequer announced a credit squeeze and put an end to any chance of us obtaining our loan.

191

It was a great disappointment to me, particularly just when I thought I was at least going to move in the right direction, if a little way out. But it was not to be.

Having sold the house, we decided to buy a business which we could both run and which would enable us to be with the children all day. We were very much a nuclear family. I would have preferred to still be part of an extended family but it was the way things had evolved.

The business which we found was on the Kent coast. Sixty miles away seemed a great distance but I had been isolated when only six miles away so I was not particularly bothered. When we lost the haberdasher's shop I had given up hope of ever returning to the area where my roots lay.

So, the house was sold, we bought a car and off we went to the Kent coast.

It really was good fun building up the business and getting to know the area. We had moved at the beginning of the summer and the children were able to spend a lot of time on the lovely sandy beach which was not far from the shop.

Within a couple of years most of our friends had acquired cars and we were not short of visitors. The children were at school but still a great deal of time was spent on the beach. But although we enjoyed building up the business, it was very hard work and I would not recommend it, one makes good customers who are friendly but very few close friends. Our business was an off-licence, before the opening hours became as liberal as they now are. But it suited us. It enabled us to spend the afternoons as a family and to work during the evening when the children were in bed. Our customers were lovely people who supported us.

I would make the occasional visit to London by train. As with most things, there was a routine. My mother would meet me at Charing Cross. Coffee in the Lyons cafeteria opposite the station. Walk to Piccadilly Circus, up Regents Street, along Oxford Street to Marble Arch, lunch in Lyons

Corner House, walk back to Oxford Circus, bus home to parents' house, have tea, journey back to Charing Cross station in my father's car and train back to Kent. It never varied and the highlight of the day for my mother was the great length of time we would always spend in Selfridges' basement kitchen department.

For the first year my husband would drive up to London for two days each month to work and thereby supplement our income while we were building up the business.

The very nice accommodation was large, comprising shop and living space downstairs plus a two-floor apartment above the shop, which was reached after journeying through various storerooms to the 'front' door. This 'front' door was at the side, as was the garage door, because the shop occupied a corner site.

Until great alterations were made enabling the kitchen to be installed in the living space downstairs, we used the kitchen in the upstairs flat, which made for difficulties during the two days when my husband was away. But the children and I made a game of it. They were not of school age so were on hand to help. Well, the four-year-old helped and the younger just joined in the fun.

I would stand the elder girl on a chair, enabling her to reach the telephone, while I ran through the storerooms and up to the apartment. If a customer came into the shop, she would pick up the telephone and ping it to the extension upstairs and I would go down to serve the customer, passing on the way down daughter number two, who was still making her way up the stairs, following me and repeating, 'Wait for me.' Whereupon she would be scooped up and taken back downstairs.

Cooking the lunch gave me plenty of exercise and, as I have already said, we made the whole thing into a game. But this was only necessary for one year because the business soon began to prosper. That was a difficult two days every month but the customers were wonderful. They were all regular customers, because the shop was not in the high street but in a built-up residential area close to a hospital, the staff of which also supported us very well.

We employed an elderly gentleman to assist me in the shop in the evenings during those two days, but it was the consideration of the customers which I found so helpful at that time. They seemed to appreciate the fact that we were very young and our children were only two and four years old. When my husband returned from London they would call to the children, who were already dressed in their pyjamas ready for bed, that their daddy was home.

I do not think that I would feel happy for a young lady to be left in charge of an off-licence at the present time. To serve until 10.30 p.m., then lock up for the night, take charge of the day's takings and remain with two very small children alone on the huge premises would not be my idea of fun nowadays. But things were different then, with less crime, no drug-taking that the majority of the population were aware of and, although people purchased their drinks from us, be they soft or alcoholic, they were taken home before being consumed. We would not have allowed anyone to stand outside our shop drinking. We owned the shop for about eight years and never ever had a problem. Has the easing of our licensing laws really been advantageous when one studies the results?

But after a year the need for my husband to supplement our income by working for two days a month in London ceased and the shop became very busy. It was a very happy time. The children settled in well, as children always will, given the opportunity. They had school, church, Brownies, etc., but as a family we only made friends with one other family and they moved away. Our friends were still where we had left them and I still missed them.

After five years the novelty began to wear off. The

194

incentive was no longer there. It became a case of just ordering stock and selling it. So, we decided to move out and employ a manager to run the off-licence, and my husband returned to his own profession. A few years later we moved to Canterbury.

During these years and those following, my parents continued to live in the same house. My father had long since bought the adjoining piece of land to the side of his house which had been the end of the baker's garden and had built his garage on it. The house was continually visited by my brother and me and our families. Grandchildren would visit and stay there quite often.

I would drive up with the children at school holiday time and make my parents' house our base for visiting friends and relatives, often accompanied by my mother, whose company I never tired of – she was always such good fun.

Traffic was not as heavy then as it is now and the girls and I would often go up to visit just for the day, very rarely getting in a traffic jam if we steered clear of the London rush hour.

I probably made a mistake in adhering to my family and old friends but this was not deliberate. Life has never been dull, I have always been involved in a variety of activities, particularly studying, but my roots are still in London and with my old friends.

We have all passed the stage when we were 'home' to our families made up of children and grandchildren. Our children have now become the nucleus for their families, which inevitably leaves us in most cases to be the oldest family members. Now is the time when the oldest of friends need each other's company the most.

*

Here seems a good point in this narrative to chronicle the existence of a 'club' which was started by the new vicar's wife forty years ago. She decided not to call it a 'young wives' club' – which was the title used by most churches at that time. Because we met every Wednesday evening at 8 o'clock it was and still is called the 8 o'clock club.

While her husband was our vicar we met in the vicarage. Often he would cycle to my home to watch an important football match on television with my husband rather than watch it in his own home to the accompaniment of the 8 o'clock club chatter in the adjoining room. Now we meet in the church hall.

We are getting older and our numbers are declining. Some members have moved away to be nearer their children, others sadly have died, but there are about twelve who still meet regularly. We either have a speaker or a DIY evening, which covers a variety of topics. The subject might be a particular colour, an event or a well-known person and it is amazing the assortment of information and artefacts which are produced during one of these evenings.

But what is so important and unusual about this small group of ladies is the companionship which exists between us. We are able to disclose and discuss our innermost thoughts, worries, beliefs, etc. in the most open and frank way, in the knowledge that the help our friends will return, be it by prayer or advice, will be genuine to a fault.

I am very fortunate indeed to belong to this small group of friends. Without them life away from my old friends would indeed be even more lonely.

When my parents were about seventy years of age we all decided the time had come for them to move away from London to be near us in Kent. My brother and his family had also settled in Kent. I am not certain why we all thought this such a good idea because they were still very comfortable in their home and very active. They still had their car and therefore were able to visit friends and relatives. They also attended evening classes, Mum to do her dressmaking and Dad his painting with water colours.

I would still stay with them during my school holidays and we would go visiting together during the day. In the evenings Mum and I would spend happy hours sitting with the same 'Auntie', Mum's old school friend who still lived in No. 3 and who had shared our Anderson shelter. After all those years I still enjoyed listening to those two good friends chatting and, believe it or not as you wish, I actually heard the ending of the original scandal, the beginning of which I had heard, unbeknown to them both, when I was fifteen. It seems that after thirty years the scandal was resolved by an unexpected happy ending.

We eventually persuaded both my mother and father that it would be advantageous to all if they moved nearer to us. Details of properties were sent to me by local estate agents and we informed Mum and Dad of any that were suitable. They actually journeyed down a couple of times to view properties and we all believed them to be serious in their intent. It was after Dad's death that Mum told me that he had not wanted to move and continued showing an interest only to 'keep me happy'.

One day details of the perfect house for their requirements arrived. It could not have been more suitable in any way: modern, with a garage, in the town centre, close to the bus station and adjacent to the railway station. Suddenly, to my surprise, when I explained all this on the telephone they arranged to view the property the next day. They saw the house and decided to buy it.

They sold their London home and all went smoothly, culminating in their settling in their new home. But it must have been a dreadful wrench for them both to leave not only the area where they were both born and had lived all their lives, but also to leave the house in which they had begun their married life fifty-two years before and in which my father had lived for seventy-four years. He had spent his childhood in it, bought it, improved it in many ways and maintained it for so long, and yet I cannot remember any of us commenting on this at the time of their move. I have this feeling of guilt that I did not utter at least a few words of sympathy to him, knowing how I feel about my 'roots'.

The size of his new garage enabled him to take a great many of his tools and much of the paraphernalia collected over a lifetime, but a lot had to be disposed of rather quickly and he must have been very sad.

They settled in really well, immediately joining various activities. Unfortunately Dad died four months later. Mum believed he was aware that he was ill and this had been the reason for his sudden acceptance of the move. Maybe, I will never know. If she was correct, he may have been more contented of mind knowing they were living close to their children, particularly if he thought she might soon be left living alone.

When Dad died he was seventy-five years of age. Mum was seventy-four, but she was a very active seventy-four and she set about making a new life without him. With wonderful neighbours and friends at her clubs, she settled down very well. She always was a home-maker, both my parents were, and soon her new home was unbelievably cosy and welcoming. But she never forgot her friends and relations in London, particularly her school friend who had lived two houses away. Until well in her eighties she would journey by coach to Victoria coach station, walk to the front entrance of Victoria main line station and from there complete the journey by bus to visit her friend. She would stay overnight and next day do the return trip by bus and coach.

I understand exactly how she felt about seeing her friend because for forty years I have been driving up to visit mine.

As well as her solo trips, I would regularly drive Mum to London and Essex, enjoying the visits just as much as she did. Now and again we would stay in a hotel and spend a few days visiting and searching out the graves of her parents, her brother, Auntie Nellie's twins and various old friends. Incidentally, I do not regard this at all morbid and still visit the various cemeteries when I am in those districts to find the graves of persons I loved. I consider myself very fortunate to have been always well informed as to the resting places of those I loved and a few who died young, before I was born, but whom my parents loved. Just to stand by their graves and reflect on past times in those locations I find a very peaceful experience.

I now have to make the journey alone. My friends and I enjoy a lovely day together and the following morning I brave the M25 to journey to Auntie Nellie, with whom I spend the day before returning home.

On one of these recent visits my aunt commented that the only person missing from her large display of photographs was her beloved elder brother who had died so young. I knew I possessed a copy of the photograph which was set in his headstone. It gave me great joy to be able to have a copy made and mounted for her. It gave her even greater joy when she received it. She telephoned to tell me that every time she looked at it she cried happy tears.

I am not very religious in the sense that I go to church every Sunday to meet like-minded persons. I am not over fond of all the pomp and ceremony which the church sets store by and I cannot equate these practices with the way Jesus led his life. I can never bring myself to blame God for the things which go wrong. I believe he did all that can be expected of him by giving me life and the free-will to live it

199

as I choose. However, having said that, I must admit to always thanking him when things go well and telling him how puzzled I feel sometimes when something goes horribly wrong.

I consider my relationship with God as purely personal, hence the reason for my not feeling the need for the fellowship of a church service, but taking Holy Communion is the church service which I like the best.

I believe a mother should go to church to thank God for the birth of her baby, but I am sceptical as to whether many attend this little thanksgiving service now. Children should go to Sunday school quite simply to learn about God. We are now a multi-cultural society. I am writing as a Christian, but to whichever faith one belongs there are similar customs which should be observed to set children on the right moral path in life.

Although I do not feel myself to be terribly religious, the final resting place for my remains is of great importance to me and in this respect I am not happy.

Earlier in this narrative I made reference to two poems which mean a great deal to me. The second I discovered while studying for my School Certificate at the age of fifteen, and it made a great impression on me then which the years have not diminished. When I tell you, the reader, that the poem is *The Soldier* by Rupert Brooke you will understand that the question of one's final resting place is not only important to me now but I believe always has been.

If I should die, think only this of me:
    That there's some corner of a foreign field
That is forever England. There shall be
    In that rich earth a richer dust concealed;
A dust whom England bore, shaped, made aware,
    Gave, once, her flowers to love, her ways to roam,

200

A body of England's, breathing English air,
    Washed by the rivers, blest by suns of home.

And think, this heart, all evil shed away,
    A pulse in the eternal mind, no less
Gives somewhere back the thoughts by England given;
    Her sights and sounds; dreams happy as her day:
And laughter, learnt of friends; and gentleness,
    In hearts at peace, under an English heaven.

I always thought it sad that those soldiers' final resting place should be in a foreign place and not in their homeland.

When my father died, as so often happens, the shock was great and decisions were made quickly. He was cremated and his ashes rest in the local crematorium.

If only I had thought about it more deeply I would have suggested to my mother and brother that, after the cremation, we took Dad's ashes to Manor Park Cemetery in London to rest. I know Dad would have preferred that. We could have taken Mum's ashes to be put with his seventeen years later.

As it is now, my ashes at some future date will be put with theirs. But I would have preferred it if my final resting place was going to be with them and our family and friends. However, I will be with my dear Mum and Dad.

When we travelled up to London recently to attend the funeral of the aunt for whom I would baby-sit when her husband was serving in Ceylon during the Second World War, one cousin remarked that once we all met at family weddings but now, with weddings not as popular as they once were, we only seem to get together at funerals.

But at least we can be relied upon to do that, which is more than some families can.

When my father died, my mother's relatives and friends as well as his, made the seventy-mile journey from London and Essex to attend his funeral, and when Mum died not only her relatives but my paternal cousins and their husbands made the same journeys. It shows a great deal of respect by all and I am indeed fortunate to be part of two such close-knit families.

Maybe after so long away I should think of home as being where I now live. But no, home is where my roots are, and for me that is London – and I know now that I will never go home.